COMBAT AIRCRAFT

## 142 RAF TORNADO UNITS IN COMBAT
## 1992–2019

SERIES EDITOR TONY HOLMES

# 142

## COMBAT AIRCRAFT

Michael Napier

# RAF TORNADO UNITS IN COMBAT 1992–2019

OSPREY
PUBLISHING

OSPREY PUBLISHING
Bloomsbury Publishing Plc
Kemp House, Chawley Park, Cumnor Hill, Oxford, OX2 9PH, UK
29 Earlsfort Terrace, Dublin 2, Ireland
1385 Broadway, 5th Floor, New York, NY 10018, USA
Email: info@ospreypublishing.com
**www.ospreypublishing.com**

OSPREY is a trademark of Osprey Publishing Ltd

First published in Great Britain in 2022
© Osprey Publishing Ltd, 2022

A catalogue record for this book is available from the British Library.

ISBN: PB 9781472850249; eBook 9781472850256;
ePDF 9781472850263; XML 9781472850270

22 23 24 25 26 10 9 8 7 6 5 4 3 2 1

Edited by Tony Holmes
Cover Artwork by Gareth Hector
Aircraft Profiles by Janusz Światłoń
Index by Zoe Ross
Originated by PDQ Digital Media Solutions, UK
Printed and bound in India by Replika Press Private Ltd

Osprey Publishing supports the Woodland Trust, the UK's leading woodland
conservation charity.

To find out more about our authors and books visit **www.ospreypublishing.com**.
Here you will find extracts, author interviews, details of forthcoming events and
the option to sign up for our newsletter.

**Acknowledgements**
I am very grateful to the following ex-Tornado aircrew for their help in preparing this
book – Timo Anderson, Dave Armstrong, Steve Barnes, Chris Bearblock, Stan
Boardman, Nick Bury, Iain Cosens, Chris Coulls, Ian Davis, Steve Dean, Ian Dornan,
Trev Dugan, Paul Froome, Kev Gambold, Andy Glover, David Hales, Richard
Hartley, Simon Hulme, Jameel Janjua, James Klein, Robbie Low, Gus MacDonald,
Gordon Niven, Andy Robins, John Robins-Walker, Pete Rochelle, Phil Rossiter, Mark
Royce, Kev Rumens, 'Kiwi' Spencer, Chris Stradling, Bev Thorpe and Larry Williams.

**Front Cover**
Under the contrails from the ALARM
missiles fired moments earlier by the
formation, Tornado ZD793 flown by Sqn Ldr
K Rumens and Flt Lt T Carr releases its load
of Enhanced Paveway II weapons on a
Republican Guard barracks to the
southwest of Baghdad during a dawn strike
on 21 March 2003 as part of Operation
*Telic* (*Cover artwork by Gareth Hector*)

**Previous Pages**
The desolate mountains of Afghanistan
make an interesting backdrop to Tornado
GR 4 ZA589 on an Operation Herrick
mission. The aircraft is armed with a DMS
Brimstone missile and a 500-lb Paveway IV
LGB (*Chris Stradling*)

# CONTENTS

# INTRODUCTION

onceived at the height of the Cold War in the 1970s as the Multi-Role Combat Aircraft, the Panavia Tornado entered Royal Air Force (RAF) service in the mid 1980s in two versions, an all-weather low-level strike/interdiction aircraft (the Tornado GR 1) and an all-weather long-range interceptor (the Tornado F 3). The end of the Cold War, marked by the fall of the Berlin Wall in November 1989, was followed by Gulf War I, in which both versions of the Tornado saw action using tactics that had not been foreseen during the days of the Cold War.

Gulf War I marked a paradigm shift in RAF operations. Instead of fighting from prepared positions in Europe, the Tornado ground attack and air defence forces found themselves over the next 28 years involved in expeditionary warfare across the Balkans, the Middle East and North Africa. It says much about the aircraft that it spent more than three-quarters of its frontline service involved in active operations, carrying out roles for which it was not originally intended. In short, the Tornado truly was a Multi-Role Combat Aircraft.

The deployment of the Tornado in the RAF reached its apogee in 1990, when the type equipped 11 strike/attack squadrons (of which eight were based in Germany) and seven air defence squadrons. However, the Options for Change defence review carried out that year resulted in the disbandment of Tornado GR 1 squadrons based at Laarbruch, in Germany, and the transfer of two squadrons from

Tornado GR 4 ZA449 holds station off the port wing of a Royal Australian Air Force KC-30A tanker over Iraq after refuelling in January 2015. By the time the type was withdrawn from service in March 2019, the RAF's Tornados (GR 1, F 3 and GR 4 variants) had undertaken 28 years of continuous deployed operations since the end of Gulf War I (*Australian Department of Defence*)

Marham, in Norfolk, to Lossiemouth, in Scotland, to convert to the anti-shipping role.

For the next 29 years, the operational focus of the Tornado ground attack squadrons was in the Middle East, with the Tornado GR 1 (and later GR 4) squadrons being involved in operations over Iraq, Afghanistan, Libya and Syria continuously from 1992. Meanwhile, the Tornado F 3 squadrons maintained operational Quick Reaction Alert (QRA) in Britain and the Falkland Islands, and also undertook deployments that saw jets patrol over the Balkans, the Baltic and Iraq.

After the re-organisation that followed the Options for Change review, the Order of Battle of the RAF Tornado Force was as follows in 1992;

| RAF Germany | | |
|---|---|---|
| Brüggen | No 9 Sqn | Tornado GR 1 |
| | No 14 Sqn | Tornado GR 1 |
| | No 17 Sqn | Tornado GR 1 |
| | No 31 Sqn | Tornado GR 1 |
| **RAF Strike Command** | | |
| **No 1 Group** | | |
| Marham | No 2 Sqn | Tornado GR 1A |
| | No 13 Sqn | Tornado GR 1A |
| **No 11 Group** | | |
| Coningsby | No 5 Sqn | Tornado F 3 |
| | No 29 Sqn | Tornado F 3 |
| Leeming | No 11 Sqn | Tornado F 3 |
| | No 23 Sqn | Tornado F 3 |
| | No 25 Sqn | Tornado F 3 |
| Leuchars | No 43 Sqn | Tornado F 3 |
| | No 111 Sqn | Tornado F 3 |
| **No 18 Group** | | |
| Lossiemouth | No 12 Sqn | Tornado GR 1B |
| | No 617 Sqn | Tornado GR 1B |

A Mid-Life Update (MLU) in the late 1990s saw the Tornado GR 1 airframes being modified to Tornado GR 4 standard, which, amongst other things, gave the aircraft a full capability to employ 'smart' weapons such as the MBDA Storm Shadow and Dual-Mode Seeker (DMS) Brimstone missiles. The Tornado F 3 also saw continuous upgrades to its operational capability, including the Combat Sustainability Programme (CSP) in the early 2000s that introduced the new Link 16 Joint Tactical Information Distribution System (JTIDS) network as well as the capability to use the Advanced Short Range Air-to-Air Missile (ASRAAM) and Advanced Medium Range Air-to-Air Missile (AMRAAM) systems. However, throughout their post-Cold War career, both variants of the Tornado were limited by the pedestrian performance at medium-level of the airframe and their Turbo-Union RB199 engines.

Squadron disbandments gradually reduced the Tornado GR 1/4 force from eight squadrons in 1992 to just three by 2018. When the Tornado GR 4 ceased operations in March of the following year to make way for the Lockheed-Martin F-35 Lightning, the Tornado F 3 had already been phased out of service in favour of the Eurofighter Typhoon, with the last unit, No 111 Sqn, disbanding in March 2011.

## CHAPTER ONE

# IRAQ 1992–99

## OPERATION *JURAL*

At the end of Gulf War I, the United Nations (UN) had established a No-Fly Zone (NFZ) over northern Iraq in order to protect the Kurdish population from air attack by the Iraqi regime. The NFZ effectively prevented Iraqi forces from operating any aircraft north of the 36th Parallel. RAF Jaguars had been deployed to the Turkish base at Incirlik as part of the British contribution to air operations (known as Operation *Warden*). By mid-1992, it was apparent that a similar arrangement was needed to protect the Shi'ite Arabs in southern Iraq from punitive operations by Iraqi government forces.

Originally, it was envisaged that the British contribution to this new NFZ would comprise a small number of Tornado GR 1A reconnaissance aircraft, which would operate at low-level in much the same way as they had done, with great success, in Gulf War I. They would be used to gather intelligence about, and to monitor, Iraqi ground forces, while US and French fighters prevented the Iraqi Air Force (IrAF) from flying south of the 32nd Parallel.

Unfortunately for this plan, the US leadership of the Coalition formed to undertake this operation had already decreed that no aircraft were to operate below 10,000 ft. The Tornado Infra-Red Reconnaissance System had been specifically designed for low-level operations, so it was quickly apparent that the Tornado GR 1A was the wrong platform to use. Instead, the two existing GEC-Ferranti Thermal Imaging Airborne Laser

Wearing the Desert Pink camouflage originally used during Operation *Granby* (Gulf War I) and the markings of No 617 Sqn, Tornado GR 1 ZA470 is carrying a TIALD pod during an Operation *Jural* sortie over southern Iraq in December 1992 (*Author's Collection*)

Designator (TIALD) pods would be used by Tornado GR 1s as 'mobile security cameras' to film activity on the ground below the NFZ. The US/Coalition operation was known as Operation *Southern Watch*, and the British participation was codenamed Operation *Jural*. Six Tornado GR 1s from No 17 Sqn deployed to Dhahran, in Saudi Arabia, in August 1992 to commence operations.

The prototype TIALD pods used during Gulf War I had been replaced in service by two early production pods – these were despatched to Dhahran, where they were known as 'Becky' and 'Rachel'.

The daily Operation *Jural* routine was to mount an operational four-ship made up of two pairs, each in turn comprising a TIALD-armed reconnaissance aircraft and a 'shooter' escort. All aircraft carried live guns and missiles. Once in Iraqi airspace, the four-ship would split into its constituent pairs to cover the reconnaissance task. Each TIALD aircraft was allocated a number of 'points of interest' in Iraq to film, as well as various line searches following roadways through the marsh area to the south of the Euphrates River and to the east of the southern reaches of the Tigris River.

At medium level, and with the navigator very much 'heads in' while monitoring the TIALD picture, the reconnaissance aircraft was vulnerable to attack either by fighter aircraft or SAMs, hence the need for the 'shooter' escort. In practice, the four Tornados would make up only part of a much larger Coalition package operating within the NFZ, and there was an almost continuous presence of Coalition air defence aircraft such as USAF F-15C Eagles and *Armée de l'Air* Mirage 2000Cs.

Each squadron was responsible for providing crews for a three-month period, but rather than the entire unit deploying for the whole period, a system of 'roulement' was introduced whereby crews were cycled through Dhahran for a six-week tour. Staggered starting dates for each pair of crews meant that there would be a continuous presence of locally experienced pilots and navigators. No 617 Sqn took over from No 17 Sqn, which, in turn, handed over to No 14 Sqn in November 1992.

Describing a mission flown on 16 December, one pilot detailed a typical task for an Operation *Jural* sortie. This involved flying 'across to the marshes to run up the road to Al Amarah, then back across the marshes, back up to Al Amarah to check out a barracks, across to look for a SA-2 SAM site in the middle of the desert, down to Nasiriyah to look for another troop concentration and then home'. A flight like this would last around three hours.

The winter weather was not altogether helpful for reconnaissance operations, and sorties frequently had to be curtailed or re-tasked when cloud obscured the ground. Nevertheless, the Tornado detachment flew nearly every day. This included Christmas and New Year's Days, which was a new experience for crews used to the festive stand-downs of the Cold War! As a result, most crews flew about 40 hours a month during the detachment – well over twice the typical total for flying at Brüggen.

The high tempo of operations and relatively long sortie lengths swiftly brought up the landmark of 1000 hours flown by Tornado GR 1s on Operation *Jural*. This milestone was achieved on 29 November during the first trip in-theatre by Flt Lts D K Roxburgh, D J A Potter, K A Ward and Flg Off L P Williams of No 14 Sqn.

Although Coalition forces enjoyed air supremacy over southern Iraq, the Iraqi forces still represented a credible threat to individual aircraft operating in the NFZ. There were SA-3 SAM sites around some of the larger airfields, for example Basrah and Tallil, which were 'no-go areas' for Coalition aircraft, and Iraqi air defence radars monitored operations in the NFZ. IrAF fighters also periodically flew into the NFZ in the hope, perhaps, of finding an unescorted reconnaissance aircraft. It was for this reason that Coalition aircraft were always armed and flew in pairs while over Iraq.

The daily reconnaissance task had become routine by mid-December, but there were strong indications that the Iraqis intended to contest the NFZ. SAM systems were deployed south of the 32nd Parallel and, later in the month, IrAF fighters began to make high-speed dashes into the NFZ. Then, on 27 December, an IrAF MiG-25 was shot down by an American F-16D Fighting Falcon – the first air-to-air kill both for a USAF F-16 and for an AIM-120 AMRAAM. Although reconnaissance tasks continued, planning started for an air attack by Coalition aircraft to force the Iraqis to withdraw their air defence systems from the NFZ.

## OPERATION *INGLETON*

On the evening of 13 January 1993, a force of around 100 Coalition aircraft, including escort and support aircraft, set out from airfields in Saudi Arabia and Bahrain and from the aircraft carrier USS *Kitty Hawk* (CV-63) sailing in the Northern Arabian Gulf, to attack the nodal points of the Iraqi air defence system south of the 32nd Parallel. Known SA-3 sites in the NFZ were also targeted. The RAF contribution to the action, codenamed Operation *Ingleton*, comprised four Tornado GR 1s led by Sqn Ldr M J W Napier and Flg Off C Platt. The aircraft operated in two pairs, each comprising a bomber armed with three Paveway II 1000-lb Laser-Guided Bombs (LGBs) and a 'spiker' equipped with a TIALD pod.

This first Operation *Ingleton* mission was tasked against the Al Amarah Integrated Operations Centre (IOC) – a large complex near Musay'idah, about ten miles south of the city of Al Amarah itself. The targets within the IOC included the headquarters building, several control bunkers and a number of radar systems and radio relay antennae. The lead pair of Tornados was detailed to attack the headquarters building, while the target for the second pair was a radar control bunker. Other targets within the complex would be dealt with by USAF and US Navy assets.

After air-to-air refuelling (AAR) from a Bahrain-based Victor K 2 tanker, the Tornados crossed the border. Flt Lt C D Bearblock, the No 3 pilot, described his experiences of the mission;

'The first bombs to go off will be the big American strike on Tallil as we pass to the east. Eyes left and five, four, three, two, one. FLASH. Wow! The whole night sky lights up right on zero hour with the flash of multiple bomb explosions. It's the most impressive sight I've ever seen. I discuss with Taff [Bearblock's navigator], "They know we're coming now; expect to see the RHWR [Radar Homing and Warning Receiver] light up". For the first time the flight ceases to be like all other training missions – this time they're really going to shoot at us!

A pair of Desert Pink Tornado GR 1s refuel from a Victor K 2 of No 55 Sqn prior to 'pushing' into the southern NFZ for an Operation *Jural* mission in late 1992 or early 1993. The last of the Victor K 2s were retired when No 55 Sqn disbanded on 15 October 1993 (*Author's Collection*)

'Soon afterwards the upper winds are stronger than forecast, and I start to fall behind the timeline using max dry power. The only way to catch up is to use burner, but this will be visible to all those on the ground for miles around – the Iraqis won't need radar – they'll be able to see us! We have no choice but to use it. Burner in for seven agonising seconds, all the time waiting for the RHWR to light up as the Iraqis lock onto me and "Taff". Burners out, back on the timeline. Nothing happens. Immense relief!

'"Taff" finds the IP [initial point] on the radar and all is looking good. I hear Mike and "Spiv" making all the calls between spiker and bomber that tell me that all is running to plan for the front pair. Mike calls "bombs released", and shortly after another almighty flash lights up the sky ahead of us. I hold the course steady and release our weapons in turn. I call "bombs released" and I can't turn away from the target fast enough. As I turn, I see the flashes from my bombs – great relief that they went off. I hope that they hit the target! I also see flashes of AAA, but no guidance on the RHWR – they're firing blind into the night, and all being well, we should be above it.'

From the rear cockpit of the No 4 aircraft, Flg Off C M Craghill used his TIALD pod to mark the target. 'The thermal picture was good', he reported. 'The site was easy enough to find, and we "captured" in good time. The bomber released and we started to lase. "Cookie" [Flg Off M Cook] had been giving me a countdown, but he stopped at what should have been bomb impact. I called "keep talking", to which his reply was a thoroughly helpful "keep lasing!" Then the bombs impacted, and it looked to me like they had gone short by maybe 100 ft or so, but with all the dust kicked up by the impact it was difficult to get any clear picture of the damage.

'Some time later, when a Bomb Damage Assessment [BDA] photo of the target surfaced, it showed that while the first bomb did indeed go short by 100 ft, the second was a direct hit. What had been a square building was now missing most of its eastern and southern walls.'

Five days later, on 18 January, the four Tornados flew a second mission, this time in daylight, against the radar control building at An Najaf. 'Our attack was planned from west to east, with the spiker actually running about two miles north of the NFZ on the run-in, as the target was so close to the line', recalled Flg Off Craghill. 'After release we would turn right, to be heading south, back inside the NFZ at bomb impact. We were spiker for the second pair again, the difference being that this time we would share the same target, such was its importance.

'Again, the target was easy enough to find within the site once you had the road layout memorised from target study, but the difficulty lay in actually finding the site. Our maps didn't show it very well, but the site was perched on the edge of a big ridge running north-south, forming a distinctive western boundary. As it was, on the run in to the target the lead spiker could not identify it, so they peeled off south to set up for a re-attack.

'I eventually found the target area, which showed up much better with the TV sensor than IR – an advantage of the dual-capable TIALD pod. However, as we approached the bomber's release point, I had broken out the site, but not our actual target. As I had the site layout memorised, I was confident of being able to find it, so when the bomber crew called that they were approaching release point, and "Cookie" enquired if I was "captured", I replied "No, but I will be!" Cookie cleared the bomber to release. Now the pressure was really on, and I had to nail the target. I found the entrance to the compound, followed the main road from Baghdad into the site, turned south, then back west and – bingo! There was the target.

'As "Cookie" counted down to impact time for me, I turned on the laser and waited. I actually saw the bombs come into the TIALD picture from the bottom left and blow through the sand wall surrounding the target, straight into the bunker. With three direct hits, I was confident of another kill, so I transmitted for the rest of my formation to hear "Touchdown, and the crowd goes wild!" Unfortunately, I keyed the wrong radio and the call went out on Strike Primary and was heard by every Coalition aircraft airborne! The AWACS crew responded with a confused "Uh, roger", and we headed for home.'

The crisis in southern Iraq was quickly resolved and Operation *Jural* continued with its routine. By now, No 31 Sqn had taken over the reins at Dhahran, and Wg Cdr I Hall introduced the sensible requirement that all crews practised dummy attacks as well as their reconnaissance tasks while over Iraq in order to make sure that they would be ready, if called upon again, for offensive action. Against this backdrop, Operation *Jural* remained the main focus for each squadron's activities.

In August 1994, the operational capability of the detachment was further improved with the introduction of a new reconnaissance sensor. No 14 Sqn was the first unit to use the Vinten Vicon pod – a 'traditional' photo-reconnaissance pod with high-resolution cameras, enabling crews to cover points of interest more effectively than they could with the TIALD video. Aircraft still flew in pairs, but now one carried the Vicon pod, while the other carried the TIALD pod.

## OPERATION *DRIVER*

In early October 1994, political and military tension in the Persian Gulf region increased once more after two armoured divisions of the Iraqi Republican Guard were detected moving towards the Kuwaiti border. The British response to this was Operation *Driver*, which included the deployment of six additional Tornado GR 1s to Dhahran. Brüggen was notified on 6 October to prepare to despatch the aircraft, and five days later the Tornado reinforcements, accompanied by a VC10 carrying additional ground- and aircrew, arrived in Saudi Arabia.

The new aircraft and crews commenced operations on 13 October. Operation *Driver* sorties were usually flown as six-ships, and apart from the continued reconnaissance tasking, most missions took the form of a simulated LGB attack on military installations. However, the situation died down quickly and the extra aircraft trailed home on 9 November.

## OPERATION *WARDEN*

The Tornado force also assumed responsibility for Operation *Warden* from RAF Jaguars and Harriers when those aircraft were required for operations over the Balkans in April 1995. Flying operations for *Warden* took place from the Turkish Air Force base at Incirlik, just outside Adana in the central south of the country. Without the strict Islamic laws of Saudi Arabia, and with a rather more favourable climate, Incirlik proved to be a more pleasant location than Dhahran.

The first unit to deploy there was No 617 Sqn, and over the next year the British-based units took on *Warden*, while Brüggen squadrons assumed full responsibility for *Jural*. One unfortunate effect of doubling the number of operations was to stretch the supply chain even further. Another was that rather than covering a two-month period of operations, each unit now had to cover a four-month stint.

The northern NFZ was much smaller than its southern counterpart, covering the area of Iraq north of the 36th Parallel. It included the city of Mosul and the Zagros Mountains, which marked the borders with Turkey and Iran.

The sorties over the northern NFZ followed a similar pattern to missions over southern Iraq, but there were some notable differences. Firstly, reaching the crossing point into Iraq involved a transit of nearly 500 miles eastwards along the border between Turkey and Syria, or almost twice the distance from Dhahran to the Iraqi border in the south. Secondly, the terrain was markedly different. Under the southern NFZ, the ground was virtually all at sea level, but under the northern NFZ the mountains rose to 13,000 ft. Mosul itself sat at their foot, astride the headwaters of the Tigris. However, one benefit of operations in the northern NFZ was that Iraqi forces were much less active in the area.

Tornado GR 1s refuel from a No 101 Sqn VC10K tanker over the Zagros Mountains prior to an Operation *Warden* mission into the northern NFZ in March 1996. The mountainous terrain in northern Iraq was a contrast to the low-lying desert and marshlands of the south (*Andy Glover*)

Despite the increased transit times, the smaller area of the northern NFZ meant that typical Operation *Warden* sortie lengths were about the same as those on Operation *Jural* – between two-and-a-half and three-and-a-half hours. Tanker support was provided by a VC10K, which was also based at Incirlik, and the Tornados carried out reconnaissance with both the TIALD pod and the Vicon pod over various Points of Interest. The flying was somewhat tedious, but at least the mountain scenery added some interest. 'There was no lead-in training with the [Vicon] pod', recalled Flt Lt L W Grout, who deployed with No 12 Sqn in December 1995, 'all the training being done in-theatre shadowing the in-theatre guys. It was a steep learning curve, but we cracked it'.

## OPERATION *JURAL* CONTINUES

The beginning of 1996 saw No 31 Sqn mounting Operation *Jural* from Dhahran and No 12 Sqn at Incirlik for Operation *Warden*. Perhaps the most significant event of that year from the Tornado GR 1 crews' perspective was the bombing of Dhahran's domestic accommodation site on 25 June. The truck-bomb attack, which killed a number of US personnel at the Khobar Towers complex, was carried out by Hezbollah. Thankfully, there were no British casualties, but Operation *Jural* in its entirety was moved to the Royal Saudi Air Force's Prince Sultan Air Base (PSAB) at Al Kharj, some 70 miles to the southeast of Riyadh. Here, summer daytime temperatures reached in excess of 40°C, so the working day had to start at 0230 hrs local time in order to use cooler periods.

Adorned with a squadron commander's pennant beneath the cockpit and the markings of No 2 Sqn, this Tornado GR 1 was photographed during an Operation *Warden* sortie. It is painted in the all-grey camouflage scheme that was introduced in the late 1990s, reflecting the Tornado force's shift in emphasis to medium-level operations. The aircraft is carrying a Vicon reconnaissance pod on the centreline pylon (*Andy Glover*)

This move represented a massive reduction in the quality of life for the RAF personnel on detachment in Saudi Arabia. Firstly, accommodation was in tents, which, though air-conditioned, provided little respite from either the heat of the Arabian summer or the noise of aircraft moving on a busy airfield. Secondly, there was no opportunity, as there had been at Dhahran, for short 'rest and recuperation' breaks in the more liberal and cosmopolitan atmosphere of Bahrain. As a result, morale suffered amongst all RAF personnel.

The operational flying task continued and the sortie profile for a typical Operation *Jural* mission remained largely unchanged. Some squadrons introduced a six-day working cycle for aircrews, which consisted of planning on Day 1, followed by leading the formation on Day 2, flying as No 4 on Day 3, as No 3 on Day 4, as No 2 on Day 5 and then having a day off from flying on the sixth day. However, political tension increased in the region over the summer when Iraqi forces were deployed into northern Iraq to fight Kurdish militias. In response, the US launched two cruise missile attacks on military targets in Iraq, and from August the southern NFZ was extended up to the 33rd Parallel, thus increasing the size of the area to be patrolled by Coalition aircraft.

## OPERATION *BOLTON*

Since the end of Gulf War I, the UN had been monitoring Iraq's compliance with its directives on biological and chemical warfare. The work of a team of inspectors established by the UN Special Commission (UNSCOM) had largely gone unnoticed by the media, but they were thrown into the limelight during late 1997 when the Iraqis stopped co-operating with UNSCOM.

As part of the diplomatic response to Iraq, the British initiated Operation *Bolton* in October to reinforce their presence in the region. The Saudis were unwilling to allow offensive operations to be carried out from their territory, so initially *Bolton* comprised the deployment of HMS *Invincible* (R05), augmented by the Harrier GR 7s of No 1 Sqn, to the Persian Gulf. The carrier arrived in-theatre in late January 1998.

In the meantime, however, the Kuwaiti government had expressed a willingness to host combat aircraft, and on 6 February, just three months after completing its previous operational tour, No 14 Sqn at Brüggen was given 48 hours' notice to return to the Middle East. Crews were immediately recalled from leave and detachments. After a working weekend on the station, nine Tornados left Brüggen bound for Kuwait on 9 February. A further four aircraft deployed directly from Britain.

Ali Al Salem Air Base (AAS), which lay some 25 miles to the west of Kuwait City, had been re-occupied by the Kuwaiti Air Force after Gulf War I, but details about the airfield were scant. 'The brief was pretty lean', recalled Flt Lt K R Rumens. 'We had no charts/plates and no information on radar services or approach aids. I had worked out from satellite imagery the rough runway direction and length, and it looked like concrete!'

After a seven-and-a-half hour flight, the Tornados reached Kuwait in darkness. The runway lighting showed up well, but on taxiing off the runway Flt Lt Rumens discovered that 'there were no lights anywhere else on the airfield, so we were waved off of the runway by a few engineers who had torches and we shut down and chocked nine Tornados in a tight "gaggle" on a bit of concrete just off the end of the runway. The next day in the light the engineers had to tow aircraft to

Groundcrew of No 14 Sqn pose with one of their aircraft, which is wearing the distinctive white triangular tail flash adopted during Operation *Bolton*, at AAS in Kuwait in early 1998. It was only thanks to the hardworking groundcrew that the Tornado force met its operational commitments (*No 14 Sqn Association*)

the parking places'. The airfield was still in the semi-destroyed state in which it had been left after Gulf War I.

Over the next two days, the squadron established a dispersed operating base in one of the HAS sites. Each of the large HASs had an enormous hole in the roof, thanks to the attention of Coalition aircraft during Gulf War I. Despite the holes, the HASs provided ideal storage space for engineering equipment. In one HAS, the Operations and Engineering facilities were set up inside long tents, each of which was protected with sandbags. Initially, the aircraft were parked in the open outside the HASs, but later on, as the temperatures rose, lightweight shelters were constructed to protect airframes, engineers and aircrew from the sun.

Weapons were delivered to AAS and the TIALD pods being used by No 17 Sqn for *Jural* were flown in from Al Kharj. Forty-eight hours after arriving in Kuwait, No 14 Sqn declared itself ready for operations.

In the end, the Tornado GR 1s were not needed for attack operations. Diplomatic initiatives had quickly defused the crisis, and a new agreement between Iraq and UNSCOM was signed on 17 February. However, the squadron remained at AAS for the next three months to fly *Jural*-type sorties in the southern NFZ.

Within each pair of aircraft, the TIALD-equipped leader would also be loaded with two Paveway IIs and the wingman would carry the Vicon pod. Flying continued around the clock, and most crews flew a mixture of day and night missions. When compared to Dhahran or PSAB, AAS was much closer to Iraq, resulting in considerably reduced transit times to Iraqi airspace. Sortie times were therefore shorter than on previous detachments, typically being around two hours.

As had previously been the case, Coalition aircraft also carried out practice attacks on military installations whilst in Iraqi airspace. Occasionally, the Tornados were partnered with No 1 Sqn's Harrier GR 7 aircraft, which were now operating ashore from Ahmad al-Jaber air base south of Kuwait City.

Operation *Bolton* duly subsumed Operation *Jural*, and it now included all RAF assets assigned to enforcing the southern NFZ. Thus, when No 12 Sqn took over responsibility for the Kuwait detachment in early May 1998, the Tornado GR 1 force was supporting three simultaneous operational detachments – six aircraft remained at Incirlik for Operation *Warden*, six more were at PSAB, and a further 12 were at AAS for *Bolton*.

With a full calendar of training exercises and the MLU programme in full swing, the Tornado GR 1 squadrons would be stretched to cover all the commitments. Fortunately, responsibility for Operation *Warden* was returned to the Jaguar force at the end of September 1998, which released Lossiemouth- and Marham-based Tornado GR 1 units to share the Operation *Bolton* commitment over southern Iraq.

By the time No 14 Sqn resumed Operation *Bolton* from AAS in September 1998, political tension was mounting once more after Iraq had declared the previous month that it would not, after all, co-operate with UNSCOM. Following further diplomatic activity, on 31 October Iraq announced that it would cease all forms of interaction with UNSCOM. Even so, there was very little activity below the NFZ over the next two months, making the flying over Iraq pretty dull. At the beginning of November, No 14 Sqn handed over to No 12 Sqn.

After more diplomatic manoeuvring at the UN, the Iraqis reneged on an agreement to cooperate with UNSCOM, and on 14 November the US and British governments authorised the launch of an initial wave of strike aircraft. The Tornado GR 1 crews in Kuwait had planned and briefed their mission and were just about to walk for the sortie when they were cancelled. At the last minute, Iraq had agreed to 'unconditional resumption of co-operation' with UNSCOM, so the planned air strikes were called off. However, Iraqi co-operation was short-lived, and only a month later the political tension had escalated once more

In early November, Wg Cdr S G Barnes, commanding No 12 Sqn, had taken over as detachment commander at AAS and had ensured that a number of contingency plans were in place in case the unit was called upon again for operations. 'As things progressed, and the op looked more likely', recalled Wg Cdr Barnes, 'the formation leaders were co-opted into the plan. Throughout, the squadron engineers were tremendous, producing the aircraft we needed for each wave. They moved equipment and weapons to satisfy the requirement for four aircraft per wave with TIALD pods (we only had four) where they could'.

## OPERATION *DESERT FOX*

The deadline for Iraqi compliance with the UN resolutions passed on 16 December and US and British forces were authorised to fly air strikes, which the Americans called Operation *Desert Fox*. The detachment at AAS flew three operational waves early that evening.

As there were just four TIALD pods available for all of the operational waves, only the leader and No 3 within each four-ship carried TIALD pods. Thus, within each pair, one aircraft self-designated before co-operatively designating for the wingman. The first four-ship was led by Wg Cdr Barnes, with Flt Lt J E Linter, with each aircraft armed with two Paveway II LGBs. They were tasked against the SA-3 site near Basra (with each pair attacking a different radar system within the site) and a radio relay site just to the north. The attack was planned so that the SAM site and relay station were far enough apart for each TIALD aircraft to mark two different targets.

As they neared the target area, the Tornados met with light AAA, but no missiles were fired at them. The lead aircraft attacked the SA-3 site successfully, but the No 3 aircraft's TIALD pod did not work, leaving Flt Lt Linter to use the only serviceable pod to mark both of the Desired Points of Impact (DPI) at the radio relay station.

Sqn Ldrs M Royce and L Fisher led the second wave against targets on Tallil airfield and a radio relay station just to the north at An Nasiriyah. 'The lead pair dropped a large hangar on the northern side of the airfield with three Paveway IIs and the back pair removed a pair of HASs on the southern side of the runway', wrote Sqn Ldr Royce. 'One HAS blew up quite spectacularly, turning night into day for about 20 seconds, such was the force of the residual explosion'.

In the No 4, aircraft Flg Off A Robins recalled that 'all targets were hit, including a massive secondary explosion on the HAS – a very large mushroom cloud came up to meet us, and we thought we'd hit a nuke.

Someone said, "OOH, that's gotta hurt", and we all hurriedly sped off in batwing and burner. I remember that nobody landed with any extra fuel that night. The US Navy had thoughtfully loosed off some High-Speed Anti-Radiation Missiles [HARMs] at a SA-6 site, and there was loads of AAA, as they put up a lot of stuff against us'.

It later transpired that the hangar at Tallil had contained the 'Drones of Death' – Aero L-29 Delfin jet trainers of the IrAF that were being modified as remotely piloted vehicles to carry biological weapons – and the HAS had been an ammunition store. 'Satellite imagery the following day showed scorched land and no sign of there ever having been a HAS!', reported Sqn Ldr Royce.

The third four-ship, led by Flt Lt J P Griggs and Sqn Ldr T N Harris, took off shortly after the first one. They were to attack a Republican Guard barracks at Al Kut, and once again all aircraft were armed with two Paveway IIs, with only lead and No 3 carrying TIALD pods. 'We decided we would do a "double run" guiding our own bombs, then, as soon as they impacted, switch to the target for No 4's bombs, which were already in the air', reported Sqn Ldr D Armstrong, who was flying the No 3 aircraft. 'In the event, this was a bad idea – not enough time to get fixed on the second target, and too much pressure on our own target run knowing the bombs were already flying'.

The sortie also ended with some excitement. 'Our leader got Roland launch warnings linked with a flash on the desert floor as we approached the Kuwaiti border on the way home', continued Sqn Ldr Armstrong. 'He immediately went into his evasive manoeuvre and banged the wing tanks off. "Jez" said it was the longest two seconds of his life after he hit the jettison button!' As it turned out, the flash on the desert floor was caused by US Navy aircraft dropping their weapons on a 'dump' target, which the RAF detachment was unaware of because of communications difficulties with the American ships. It also transpired that a simultaneous SA-3 warning was spurious too, having been caused by microwave links in the desert. 'The engineers gave "Jez" the bill for the tanks', added Armstrong.

In the meantime, six crews from No 617 Sqn deployed to AAS on 17 December to support the operations. 'We arrived just after the first trip had taken off, and we awoke the next morning to the participants mooching about, having faced the reality of combat', remembered Sqn Ldr A K F Pease. 'Those of us who deployed from No 617 Sqn were not used in anger, and having deployed thinking we would be away for a couple of months, we actually got home in time for Christmas, which was a bonus!'

On the second night of the operation, 18 December, the Tornado waves were launched with enough time spacing between them so that all aircraft could carry a TIALD pod and self-designate their own targets. In turn, this allowed for a much more compressed attack to be flown. Wg Cdr Barnes led his formation against the SA-3 site at Tallil, attacking its 'Low Blow' and 'Perfect Patch' radars and two HQ buildings within the complex. Once again, the attackers were met with very light AAA and no SAMs were fired. When summarising the mission, Wg Cdr Barnes stated that 'the plan "ran on rails" and all DPIs were hit successfully'.

'Night 2 saw us doing a coordinated bombing run on the Al Kut Republican Guard barracks', recalled Sqn Ldr Royce, 'with a whole bunch of US bombers and the standard SEAD [Suppression of Enemy Air Defences] and fighter escorts. The Guards sent up quite a fierce AAA defence, but no missiles – I'm sure the EW assets had neutralised whatever they may have had to hand; I'd never seen so many HARMs fired at one sitting'. Once again, however, the difficulty in coordinating with the US Navy was illustrated when the formation of carrier aircraft ahead of the Tornados slipped back on their Time-on-Target. 'We later calculated that their bombs were within ten seconds of dropping through our formation/canopies and hitting the lead aircraft', reported Flg Off Robins.

The third wave carried out their attack in the early hours of 19 December. This successful mission, led by Flt Lt Griggs and Sqn Ldr Harris, was also tasked against targets in the Al Kut area.

On the third night of operations, the Tornados were armed with the new Paveway III 2000-lb weapon. 'DPIs were running out, and I had argued (forcibly) with HQ that some of the targets were not worth risking lives over', recalled Wg Cdr Barnes. 'I had proposed sending a two-ship only, but we were re-allocated more sensible targets. The target area was Al Kut, close to the 32nd Parallel, and the targets were "Low Blow" and "Perfect Patch" radars and two HQ buildings – déjà vu.

'There were real problems with coordination, as we couldn't contact the carrier. We didn't get the correct details and we ended up doing our own thing, deconflicted by height and time, but running in a clockwise direction, with the rest of the package going the opposite way. There was a lot of AAA en route, and particularly in the target area. SEAD reported some missiles fired at the package, but I did not see any. Three DPIs were hit, and No 3 guided his weapon safely into open desert, having misidentified the target.

'I think this was the first operational use of Paveway III, and at the very least we validated tactics and procedures with this weapon. The groundcrew piped me into the shelter on our return [piper standing on top of the cab of one of the tractors], which was very emotional.'

A second wave led by Sqn Ldr Royce took off shortly after the first wave. This formation, tasked against bunkers and another radio relay station just outside Basra, was also loaded with Paveway IIIs. However, the mission was cancelled before the formation crossed the border into Iraq, and the aircraft returned to AAS with their weapons.

## IRAQ AND NFZs

After a slightly delayed handover, No 12 Sqn was replaced by No 2 Sqn in Kuwait in early January 1999. Operation *Desert Fox* had been the first time that RAF aircraft had dropped bombs on targets in Iraq since the Operation *Ingleton* missions in early 1993, and it marked a massive change in policy by the Iraqi government. While it had been prepared to tolerate the southern NFZ in the post-*Ingleton* years, after *Desert Fox* the regime declared that it would no longer recognise the NFZ, and that it would engage aircraft flying over Iraqi territory. From then on attacks on Coalition aircraft became commonplace over southern Iraq, with both anti-aircraft guns and SAMs being fired.

'AAA was a big threat, and prevalent', reported Flt Lt L P Williams, a navigator with No 2 Sqn. 'There were numerous occasions when you'd suddenly notice a new cloud formation appear near to you, then realise that it was 120 mm-odd calibre AAA airburst!'

The Rules of Engagement (RoE) for British Forces were changed, and a series of Response Options (ROs) were introduced, permitting limited offensive action over Iraq. The ROs ranged from RO1, which was an attack flown in direct response to an Iraqi act of aggression, to RO5, which was a pre-planned strike against an Iraqi installation or weapon system.

A Vicon-equipped Tornado GR 1A in No 2 Sqn markings in the foreground leads a Tornado GR 1 originally from No 17 Sqn on an Operation *Bolton* sortie in 1998 (*US National Archive*)

On 31 January, No 2 Sqn aircraft led by Sqn Ldr G R Wells attacked targets at Tallil with Paveway II, and the same team followed up with two more attacks against this target on 10 and 21 February. The following day, the detachment carried out a Paveway III attack on a bunker at Ar Rumaylah. The tasking came in at short notice, and required the four-ship to be at the runway threshold ready for an immediate launch. As the day's operational wave was already airborne on a standard reconnaissance sortie, Sqn Ldr M C Alton and Flt Lt L P Williams were called in on their 'day off' to lead the mission.

'I had never even seen a Paveway III properly, let alone dropped one, and certainly had no clue about planning considerations', commented Flt Lt Williams. Nevertheless, the crew put together an effective plan, and led the formation out to the runway to wait for the word. 'After about 20 minutes at the end of the runway, the operations desk transmitted the codeword and we were off to shatter the peace and quiet of Iraq after some departing A-10s had been shot at!', continued Williams. 'One big factor was the wind. We had already planned to use the tailwind (Paveway III likes wind from behind), but it turned out to be easily 100 knots (rather more than we anticipated), so we had to adjust our pickle point on the target run by about two nautical miles'. Subsequent reconnaissance showed that the DPI had been hit accurately.

By now it was clear that the demands of the MLU programme were making it almost impossible for the Tornado GR 1 force to maintain six aircraft at PSAB, as well as 12 aircraft in Kuwait. Responsibility for the PSAB detachment was duly passed to the Tornado F 3 force in February 1999.

Throughout that year, Iraqi forces in southern Iraq actively sought to engage Coalition aircraft operating in the NFZ. In response, Tornado GR 1s from AAS were frequently called upon to attack Iraqi air defence elements. By August 1999 there had been more than 200 violations of the NFZ and 300 SAM launches against Coalition aircraft in the previous eight months, and in that time Tornado GR 1s had carried out air strikes against 23 targets. The pace of operations continued through the autumn and winter, and examples of so-called 'kinetic' sorties included a six-ship attack on targets at Al Kut by No 9 Sqn crews on 11 October and strikes by No 14 Sqn against S-60 AAA batteries at Al Turbak on 19 February and at Tallil on 11 March.

## CHAPTER TWO

# AIR DEFENCE OPERATIONS 1992–2011

Tornado F 3 ZE808 from No 25 Sqn
intercepts a Russian Tu-142MK 'Bear-F'
in the early 1990s. The Tornado is armed
with four AIM-9L Sidewinder AAMs
attached to the underwing stub pylons and
two Skyflash AAMs under the fuselage
(*Crown Copyright/OGL*)

## UK AIR DEFENCE (1992–2011)

Unlike the Tornado GR 1 in the nuclear strike role, the Tornado F 3 did fly operationally in its originally intended role. Throughout the aircraft's RAF service, Tornado F 3 crews maintained Quick Reaction Alert (QRA) to ensure the security of the UK Air Defence Region (UKADR) – an area of more than 2000 square miles that includes the United Kingdom and the Faroe Islands. The Northern QRA, with responsibility for the North Sea and the UK-Faroes Gap, was mounted from Leuchars, in Scotland, while the Southern QRA, which covered the southwest approaches, was mounted from Coningsby, in Lincolnshire.

Normally, two aircraft were kept fully armed with crews at RS10 (ready to launch within ten minutes) at both QRA bases, with another back-up aircraft available at RS60 (60-minute readiness). However, if intelligence sources suggested that there might be increased activity in the region, then more aircraft might be temporarily brought to high readiness. During the 1990s, the Long-Range Aviation of the Russian Federation Air Force was not particularly active, and there were consequently few live QRA scrambles in comparison to the Cold War years.

In the late 1990s, Southern QRA was discontinued, and with a dwindling threat to the UKADR, the number of Tornado F 3 squadrons declined steadily after 1991. No 23 Sqn was disbanded in 1994, followed by No 29 Sqn in 1998. However, following the terrorist attack on the USA on 11 September 2001, in which civilian airliners were flown into buildings, Southern QRA was re-activated at Coningsby under Operation *Adana*.

In addition to this new threat, the Russian Federation Air Force became reinvigorated early in the new century. Russian military aircraft made incursions into the UKADR on four occasions during 2005, and although there was just one incursion the next year, there were 19 in 2007. In May of that year, two Tornado F 3s were scrambled from Leuchars to intercept a Tu-95 "Bear" that was observing a maritime exercise. Four months later, in the early hours of 6 September, four Tornado F 3s were scrambled from Leeming to intercept eight Tu-95s that were approaching UK airspace. Following this spike in activity, Russian incursions settled down to around ten times per year.

Despite the increased threat level, the number of Tornado F 3 units continued to be reduced, with No 5 Sqn disbanding in 2002 and No 11 Sqn following it three years later. By 2007, the Air Order of Battle of the Tornado F 3 force was as follows;

| RAF Air Command | | |
|---|---|---|
| Leeming | No 25 Sqn | Tornado F 3 |
| Leuchars | No 43 Sqn | Tornado F 3 |
| | No 111 Sqn | Tornado F 3 |

On 10 March 2010, two Tornado F 3s from No 111 Sqn scrambled from Leuchars to intercept two Tu-160 'Blackjacks' near Stornoway. The Russian aircraft had already been intercepted in turn by fighters based in Norway, Iceland and Denmark, and the Tornados shadowed them for four hours until they turned northwards off the coast of Northern Ireland. As the squadron commander, Wg Cdr M J Gorringe, reported at the time, 'this [was] not an unusual incident. Our crews have successfully scrambled to intercept Russian aircraft on more than 20 occasions since the start of 2009'. The Eurofighter Typhoon F 2 had started to share QRA duties with the Tornado F 3 from June 2007, signalling the final rundown of squadrons equipped with the aircraft. The last Tornado F 3 unit, No 111 Sqn, was finally disbanded in March 2011.

# FALKLAND ISLANDS AIR DEFENCE (1992–2009)

In July 1992, four Tornado F 3s deployed to Mount Pleasant airfield on the Falkland Islands via Ascension Island as replacements for the soon-to-be retired Phantom FGR 2s of No 1435 Flight, which had responsibility for the air defence of the Islands. The personnel for No 1435 Flight were seconded to Mount Pleasant from other Tornado F 3 units, with groundcrew undertaking a four-month tour and aircrew completing a five-week tour of duty.

Seen at low-level over the Falkland Islands, Tornado F 3 ZG797 from No 1435 Flight has a BOL launcher rail on the inboard stub pylon and an ASRAAM on the outer (*Roy Macintyre*)

Two fully armed aircraft were kept at RS10 continuously for 365 days a year, with another crew at RS30. The QRA aircraft were supported by a VC10K tanker. Each Tornado crew worked a ten-day cycle throughout their deployment of alternating 24-hour QRA shifts and days flying training flights in the two non-QRA aircraft, followed by a day off. Sometimes, all four aircraft would be flown together. On these occasions, all four would be armed in the QRA weapons fit, and the first two to land would be refuelled and placed on RS10, whilst the other two would sit 'airborne QRA' with a tanker in support.

QRA launches were frequent to intercept Argentinian Boeing 707 or Lockheed Electra Electronic Intelligence (Elint) aircraft, although they invariably remained outside the Falkland Island Control Zone (FICZ). However, sometimes other aircraft blundered into the FICZ, including a USAF WC-135 weather reconnaissance jet that was intercepted on 25 May 1993. During the afternoon of 19 January 1999, Flt Lt R A Macintyre was called to cockpit readiness;

'Having finished strapping in, I contacted Ops via the aircraft telebrief for a situation-report. We were told an unidentified track was heading towards the Zone from the North. It was very high (66,000 ft) and doing Mach 1.6, but was following an upper air route. We were instructed to standby for further. We remained at cockpit ready for about ten minutes, during which time I considered what type of aircraft this could be, and how we were going to try and intercept it. Then a thought occurred to me, but I discounted it, thinking Ops couldn't have made such a silly mistake.

'We were told to revert to RS10. I asked what had happened, but was told Ops would call on the secure landline. Back in the Flight, I answered the phone and immediately said, "That was Concorde, wasn't it?" "How did you know?" was the reply. "Because there was an article about a South American tour in yesterday's *Daily Telegraph*!" "Oh" was the embarrassed response.'

The Air France Concorde had been routeing from Buenos Aries to Ushuaia, on Tierra Del Fuego.

'There were no low flying restrictions, and ranging across East and West Falklands at low level was the norm', wrote Sqn Ldr D J Gledhill, who commanded No 1435 Flight during 1994. 'Offshore, there were no limitations in airspace, and operations were conducted from sea level to "the moon", or as high as a "clean" F 3 would fly!

'With three control and reporting centres and a Royal Navy air defence picket ship operating off the coast, competition to control a pair of fighters was fierce. The biggest challenge was the weather – ensuring that it remained suitable to allow a recovery to the main 10,000 ft-long runway was a priority. There was a short secondary runway, but at a length of only 5000 ft, the approach from the north over Pleasant Peak could be demanding given the gusty conditions that were prevalent.'

Most Tornado F 3 aircrew could expect several stints in the Falkland Islands during their flying careers. With the impending demise of the Tornado F 3, No 1435 Flight was re-equipped with four Typhoon FGR 4s in September 2009.

## BOSNIA-HERZOGOVINA – OPERATION *DENY FLIGHT* (1993–96)

In response to the continuing civil war in the Former Yugoslavia, NATO established an NFZ over Bosnia-Herzogovina in April 1993. NATO's Operation *Deny Flight* began at noon GMT on 12 April, and it was enforced by the NATO Joint Reaction Force (JRF) comprising aircraft from Britain, the USA, France and the Netherlands. Britain's contribution to the JRF was six Tornado F 3s from No 11 Sqn, which set off for Gioia del Colle, in Italy, on 12 April. They were supported by an E-3D Sentry flying from Aviano and two VC10K tankers based at Palermo.

Initially, the Tornado F 3s were modified to a similar operational standard to that of Operation *Granby*. This meant 'Stage 1+' standard radar, Radar-Absorbent Material tiles applied to the engine air intakes in order to reduce the radar cross-section of the aircraft and a self-defence suite incorporating AN/ALE-40 flare dispensers attached to the engine access doors under the fuselage, as well as the Phimat chaff dispenser that was carried on a wing stub pylon in lieu of one AIM-9 Sidewinder.

The weapons capability included the Skyflash SuperTEMP and AIM-9M air-to-air missiles. In the front cockpit, the stick-top switches gave the pilot control over the weapons while retaining Hands On Throttle and Stick via the improved Missile Management System. Avionics updates included the permanent fitting of Havequick secure radios and a Mode 4 transponder, and the cockpits were modified to make them more compatible with Night Vision Goggles (NVGs).

Daily tasking came from Combined Air Operations Centre (CAOC) 5 at Vicenza, and the task would require pairs of Tornado F 3s to cover specified two-hour 'VUL' (vulnerable) times in the NFZ. Typically, one or two missions would be launched into the NFZ each day. For operational sorties, the aircraft were configured in 'Mike fit' with 1500-litre underwing tanks, four Skyflash and four Sidewinders. Routine sorties lasted about two hours, typically with two AAR brackets using the VC10Ks, although if the weather at the bases in Italy prevented the relief CAP from launching, the fighters might have had to remain on station for as long as five hours until the weather cleared.

One particular advantage of the Foxhunter radar in the Tornado F 3 over the AN/APG-63 fitted to USAF F-15s and F-16s that were part of the JRF was that with manual modes and a dedicated navigator to interpret it, the system was better at detecting slow-flying aircraft such as helicopters. Although a number of helicopters from both sides were intercepted, the RoE prevented any further action by the Tornado crews. However, on 13 May 1994, a pair of Tornado F 3s forced down a Croatian helicopter that had been delivering ammunition to the Bosnian Croat Army.

Operating over Bosnia was no sinecure, for Serbian anti-aircraft systems were hostile to NATO aircraft and accounted for both a Sea Harrier FRS 1, which was shot down by an SA-7 on 16 April 1994, and an F-16 downed by an SA-6 on 2 June 1995. The mountainous terrain of the country rose to some 8000 ft, while the Tornado F 3 loaded for combat missions struggled to reach 23,000–25,000 ft. Thus, the threat of man-portable infra-red guided SAMs or lock-after-launch mobile radar systems like the SA-6 was very real. Having two pairs of eyes in each aircraft to look out for SAM launches was undoubtedly an advantage for the Tornado F 3.

The operational standard of the aircraft evolved quickly in the mid-1990s. The AN/ALE-40 flare dispensers were replaced by Vinten Vicon flare dispensers, which gave an improved decoy for the Tornado F 3's engine infra-red signature. The BOL launcher rail system that included an integral chaff dispenser was also procured for the stub pylons. By using the BOL launcher rail, aircraft no longer needed to lose a weapons station in order to carry Phimat dispensers. The full war load of four Skyflash and four Sidewinder missiles could now be carried on operations.

In 1994, outer wing pylons were fitted to the Tornado F 3 in order to carry the Towed Radar Decoy (TRD, affectionately known as the 'turd'), with a Phimat chaff pod mounted on the opposite wing as a counterbalance. Fitted into the body of a BOZ-107 chaff and flare dispenser, the TRD comprised a Leonardo Ariel self-protection jammer feeding a travelling-wave tube (TWT) that was towed about 330 ft behind the aircraft. At the time it was fielded by the Tornado F 3 force, the TRD was world-leading, and the only self-protection jammer to give 100 per cent protection against certain SAM systems.

'The TWT could be jettisoned over the airfield for recovery thanks to its in-built parachute', recalled Flt Lt G P Coleman of No 29 Sqn. 'In 1994, on its first operational deployment with No 29 Sqn at Gioia, the first drop didn't go so well when the parachuting TWT drifted in the wind onto the local autostrada (Italian motorway), luckily without injury. The second recovery, having revised the procedures, was to aim at the car assigned to OC Operations Wing that had been parked to allow for the local wind. Sadly, the parachute failed to deploy, and the metal TWT scored a direct hit on the vehicle, damaging it! Subsequent recoveries worked after that'.

It is often said that air-to-air kills are like going fishing, and the experience of the Tornado F 3 crews over Bosnia certainly illustrates the analogy. In the last week of February 1994, aircraft from No 29 Sqn had been flying CAP near Udbina for ten consecutive days. They were stood down on 28 February and the aircrew were playing golf that day at the Riva de Tessali Golf Resort. 'OC 29's phone rings', recalled Flt Lt Coleman, 'and it's the CAOC. The Boss wanders into the rough with his encrypted mobile telephone. He comes back to us all – "You won't believe it!", he says. "The USAF F-16s have just bagged four out of six Serbian Jastrebs on the Udbina

Tornado F 3 ZE159 operated from Gioia del Colle during a No 43 Sqn deployment in the autumn of 1994 for Operation *Deny Flight*. The markings of its previous unit (probably No 11 Sqn, judging by the 'DE' two-letter code at the top of the fin) have been scrubbed out rather crudely (No *43 Sqn Association*)

CAP at the same time we have been there for the last ten days!" They were definitely seen as the "ones that got away" on that detachment'.

Although the Tornado F 3 crews had no luck with fixed wing aircraft, they intercepted numerous Bosnian Serb helicopters. On 11 January 1996, Flt Lts J M Goatham and Coleman were part of a pair tasked for a roving CAP over Bosnia for two hours. 'Not long into our mission the AWACS began to call an intermittent contact in the vicinity of the high ground between Zenica and Mostar, about 20 miles West of Sarajevo', reported Flt Lt Coleman.

'We committed towards the target, and it wasn't long before both of us were painting a 120-knot target tracking along a valley. We called AWACS for instructions, and the call came back "Mission Identify". As we came into visual range of the "bogey", it was quickly identified as a Mi-17 "Hip". This helicopter type was often seen on the ground shortly after going "feet dry" (i.e. coasting into hostile territory), where there were often three or four parked up on a sports field at Posusje [a short distance west of Mostar]. We knew they were flying, as sometimes you would count three to four "Hips" on the way in "feet dry", and then note there were only one or two on the way back "feet wet" for the tanker.

'On achieving visual identification of the "Hip", we requested instructions. AWACS came back with further instructions to "shadow" the "Hip" and to "report" under the orders of the CAOC 5 Air Director in Vicenza. So, between the F 3s, we set up a visually supporting orbit over the helicopter so that each aircraft had a quick weapons solution should the call to engage come.

'Reasonably quickly, the "Hip" crew spotted us setting up this offensive posture. They knew it was likely that they would not be engaged if they landed, so they landed on, and even rudely gesticulated at us in the F 3s orbiting overhead! Staying close to the ground was always dangerous, with the constant threat of unseen SA-7 engagements, so the "Hip" was monitored on the ground until we ran low on fuel and had to head to the tanker. By the time we returned the helicopter was gone and, on its way, again.'

By early 1995, the detachment at Gioia del Colle had been expanded to eight Tornado F 3s. Operation *Deny Flight* became Decisive *Endeavour* on 21 December 1995 when the NATO Implementation Force assumed responsibility for implementing the Dayton Peace Accord in Bosnia. The last Tornado F 3 detachment to fly over Bosnia was No 111 Sqn in February 1996, after which the aircraft returned to their British bases.

# IRAQ – OPERATION *RESINATE (SOUTH)* (1999–2003)

With the Tornado GR 1 force fully stretched with the prospect of simultaneous offensive operations over Iraq and Kosovo, the Tornado F 3 force stepped in to take over responsibility for Operation *Resinate (South)* and the southern NFZ. Six Tornado F 3s from No 25 Sqn deployed to PSAB in February 1999. In fact, the F 3 variant was far more suited to NFZ operations than the GR 1, since enforcement of the Zone was essentially an air defence function.

Armed with Sidewinders and Skyflash AAMs, Tornado F 3 ZE201 heads for Iraq over northern Saudi Arabia during an early Operation *Resinate (South)* sortie in 1999. Flying from PSAB, the aircraft is fitted with outboard underwing pylons and is carrying a TRD (*Gordon Pell*)

The Tornado F 3 force quickly assumed the roles of sweep/escort/ barrier CAP for the various bomber 'response options', and it also provided protection for the tankers and intelligence, surveillance, target acquisition and reconnaissance (ISTAR) assets that patrolled the Saudi border. Once again, the operational standard of the aircraft had been considerably enhanced by various modifications, including the CSP that had incorporated the JTIDS capability. JTIDS was a complete game-changer, giving Tornado F 3 crews the full picture of who was friendly and who was foe on their radar displays, thus granting them unrivalled tactical awareness.

Like the Tornado GR 1s, the Tornado F 3s were often subjected to SAM launches. The Iraqi tactic was to launch the missile 'blind' and only illuminate the target with the tracking radar once the weapon was in the air. Allegedly, President Saddam Hussein had offered a £10,000 reward for any SAM operator who shot down a Coalition aeroplane.

On 29 April 1999, Flt Lts M D Hale and Coleman were patrolling near Al Kut when the latter 'observed a SAM-2 being fired at our formation, but it did not guide to target. This was a known tactic at the time as SAM crews would launch their missiles unguided and then hope to bring up their radars long enough to get it to guide to target, prior to needing to shut it down again before a HARM from an F-16CJ *Wild Weasel* was fired back at them. The F-16CJs were not far away when the SA-2 was fired at us on that day, and so the Iraqi SAM operators had left their guidance radars off.

'As we carried out a 3D anti-SAM manoeuvre against the telegraph-pole sized missile coming up to meet us, I also released a stream of chaff and our TRD in anticipation of needing to defeat it. The F-16CJs were very excited too, expecting to reactively fire a HARM at any fire-control or missile guidance radar that might come up. In the end, the missile passed several miles away from the formation with no guidance.'

Six months later, Coleman came close to scoring an air-to-air kill;

'On 3 November 1999 we were the lead of a pair of F 3s on an OCA [Offensive Counter-Air] mission. Our callsign was "Olly' and we were assigned to BARCAP to the southwest of Baghdad – keeping any hostile aircraft from our bombers (including Tornado GR 1s), our ISTAR aircraft and the supporting tankers. Noting that we would only just have enough fuel to make the end of the VUL Time, we decided to go back to the tanker to top off with gas in case the Iraqis tried an attack at the end. It was a wise move, and as the F-15s and F-16s were turning towards the south, we were still feeding from our big 2250-litre external tanks.

'Suddenly, the AWACS started calling a group marshalling northwest of Baghdad, to the north of the 33rd Parallel (i.e. outside the NFZ). An aircraft was building speed and starting to head south towards the NFZ. We started pressing north, expecting that an attack was imminent. Again, we were not wrong. As the track crossed the 33rd Parallel, it was now supersonic, and the AWACS and other assets identified it as hostile on JTIDS. The aircraft was a MiG-23 "Flogger".

A Tornado F 3 displays the full stores and weapons fit on a *Resinate (South)* mission. A TRD is carried on the outboard port underwing pylon and a Phimat pod is carried on the opposite pylon beneath the starboard wing (*Gordon Pell*)

'I committed our formation. "'Olly', Commit, Group, 'Bull 270', 5, Medium, South, Supersonic". As I uttered the words, Russ [Sqn Ldr R M Allchorne] instinctively flicked the weapons Late Arm live switch and pushed the RB199s into Combat Power (full reheat) heading straight for the MiG. We were on our way.

'Shortly after, my JTIDS track correlated with my radar plot at around 60 miles – we were starting to close on each other at more than 22 miles per minute, so things were happening very fast. I asked Russ "shall I punch the tanks off", and he replied "Negative, let's keep them in case we need the fuel. We'll lose them after Fox 1". This was another wise call, and as we approached supersonic at more than 30,000 ft, the jet was humming and so were we with excitement.

'I told our wingman on secure voice to "remain in search, we'll lock at LSZ+2" (Launch Success Zone plus two miles). We didn't want there to be an undetected second aircraft sitting in close formation within the "resolution cell" where the radar is unable to break out the second (or more) aircraft at range. Our wingman would follow SOPs [standard operational procedures] and hold their radar in search until at about ten miles, when they too would take a lock, or sort against any other aircraft that we weren't locked to, before they launched. The beauty of JTIDS was that the wingman can see who we were locked to – we could also see their search picture – so, communication between us was minimal.

'At approximately 28 miles I took a lock against the MiG-23 about two miles from the top of the LSZ for the SuperTEMP Skyflash. The MiG-23 immediately started turning away and the LSZ shrank to about six miles in a tail chase towards the NFZ border on the 33rd Parallel – we got within about 15 miles before we had to turn away. Even if we lost the tanks, and pushed up to Mach 2.2, there wasn't enough room left to catch it inside the NFZ. We leaned away from the target and then used the fuel that we had kept, allowing us to exit the area at high speed, going back to the tanker for a top off on the way home.

'We were the last two aircraft in the NFZ at that point as the attempted attack had occurred at the end of the VUL Time and all of the other

In standard weapons fit, Tornado F 3s ZE731, ZE810 and ZE734 prepare to leave their VC10K tanker prior to entering the southern NFZ for an Operation *Resinate (South)* patrol. The Tornado F 3 took over responsibility for patrolling southern Iraq in early 1999 (*Gordon Pell*)

Coalition aircraft were either on the tanker or heading for their home bases/ships. This is believed to be the closest the F 3 ever got to firing a missile in anger – with just two to three miles to go! The whole thing lasted less than about five minutes, and we were then faced with about an hour's transit back to our base.'

For four years from February 1999 to February 2003, the Tornado F 3s flew hundreds of OCA missions to protect Coalition air assets. Each of the five Tornado F 3 units, Nos 5, 11, 25, 43 and 111 Sqns, took its turn to provide personnel for two-and-a-half-month roulements, with No 5 Sqn flying its last detachment before disbandment in February to April 2002.

As the build-up towards hostilities approached in March 2003, the detachment was expanded to 14 aircraft. The 16 crews were provided by Nos 43 and 111 Sqns of the Leuchars Wing. The aircraft were modified with the fitment of KY-100 secure radio and armed with the MBDA AIM-132 ASRAAM. The southern NFZ was divided into three lanes running north-south, each of which was covered continuously by four or eight fighters. At first, the fighters in all three lanes were co-ordinated by a Defensive Counter Air (DCA) Commander, but once hostilities started, the system proved to be too cumbersome. Instead, the fighters operated semi-autonomously within their designated lane.

'On the night of 18 March – our last Op *Resinate* mission – I was DCA Commander running 12 fighters across the three lanes when the Iraqis started launching several Mirages and MiG-23s in an apparent show of force', recalled Sqn Ldr K J Reeves from No 111 Sqn. 'Our RoE wouldn't let us go after them as they were just north of the NFZ, but I could just see them on JTIDS. Everybody in each lane had just finished the second swap out of the mission, and we had just taken over from a pair of F-15s and started our second slot when we were called to go "green" [secure radio] and were informed that at least one MiG-25 "Foxbat" had just gotten airborne opposite my lane.

'We had practised in the sim against the "Foxbat" and knew if he decided to run at the AWACS or the tankers, he would be a tricky target. The SOP would have involved "retrograding" the AWACS – getting him to run like hell, thus losing us our air picture – while we engaged the "Foxbat". Our tankers would also leg it, complicating things, as we would have to punch off our tanks to make our tiny engagement window.

'The F-15s had only just arrived on the tanker, and while they would be a formidable backstop, they needed plenty of fuel to make the intercept behind us. I called them, and told them to keep taking fuel until I called the retrograde (if the "Foxbat" decided to run south) while I watched him appear on my radar, climbing and accelerating in a huge spiral to the north. In the end, I locked him up and started an oblique run towards him, then spiked him with the CW [continuous-wave] Illuminator as he started to turn south. He got the message, probably thinking I was launching a missile at him, and arced away northwards.'

Meanwhile, in the No 3 aircraft, Flt Lt Macintyre 'watched on datalink all the US fighters abandon their lanes and rush towards the probable boundary crossing point. It was just like schoolboy football! Kenny ordered our F 3 pair back south, and we took up a goalkeeper role about 50–60 nautical miles behind the main action. We were the only unit to do this – last line of defence! We did receive plaudits for this in the mission debrief, but we glossed over the fact that we needed those 50 or so miles anyway to effect an interception against a high-flying target such as a "Foxbat"!'

## IRAQ – OPERATION *TELIC* (2003)

Operation *Telic*, which saw direct conflict with Iraq, started on 19 March 2003. The Tornado F 3 force in-theatre was tasked to fly three waves of four aircraft each day, with sortie lengths of six or seven hours. Although four aircraft were launched for each mission, only two would enter the Area of Responsibility (AOR), the other two effectively being spare airframes.

The first sorties launched before dawn and carried out AAR with NVGs, entering the AOR in the dark. Night missions were also flown, and on one of these early in the campaign, a crew from No 43 Sqn intercepted a four-ship flying low and fast over the desert. Using NVGs, the crew identified the targets as four US cruise missiles inbound from the Red Sea.

On these missions, the Tornado F 3s pushed deep into Iraq, often beyond Baghdad. Initially, operations were synchronised with pairs of F-15s to mount roving CAPs over Iraqi airfields, aiming to catch aircraft as they took off. Although the IrAF did not rise to the challenge, Coalition fighters were frequently fired upon by Iraqi SAM systems.

'We had the luxury of constantly roving and weaving, never providing a steady target', commented Sqn Ldr Reeves. 'I got a sniff of a SAM-6 tracking radar once, but it cleared as I had my finger poised over the TRD deploy button. About 20 seconds later, my wingman called the launch and we watched a smoke trail climb away. After a week or so, with no sign of Iraqi aircraft, we then switched to hunting for helicopters, roving throughout the area, often to the north of Baghdad. I chased down what I thought was a helicopter at one point, only to identify it as a silver

Fully armed with Skyflash and ASRAAM, Tornado F 3s of Nos 11 and 111 Sqns await their turn to refuel from a USAF KC-10 Extender while a B-1B replenishes its tanks during an Operation *Telic* mission on 24 March 2003 (*Kenneth Reeves*)

Armed with ASRAAM and AMRAAM and equipped with JTIDS, the Tornado F 3 had matured into an extremely capable and effective weapons platform by the early 2000s (*Roy Macintyre*)

Mercedes doing about 130 mph towards the Jordanian border'.

Flt Lt Macintyre flew ten operational missions, the first of which was at night. 'Our particular datum that night', he later recalled, 'was about 25 miles southwest of Baghdad, and to me the city looked totally on fire. I could see explosions going off all around the city as weapons impacted. At this point, there was very little activity on the ground outside of the capital. We had great situational awareness from the E-3 picture via datalink that there was no airborne threat. The biggest danger to us was a blue-on-blue collision.

'About half an hour into the task, I remember calling out to my nav, "My God, someone has just gone in", as I saw a light dive towards the city centre and then an explosion. A few moments later, I saw the same thing happen again. It was then that I realised I was seeing the terminal flight phases of cruise missiles!'

Although the Tornado F 3s mainly tasked into the central lane, on occasions they were switched into the eastern lane in response to Iranian activity, or to the western lane to provide cover for Coalition Scud missile hunters. Rather than directly supporting individual strike packages, the Tornado F 3s sanitised the whole area being used by Coalition ground attack aircraft. CAPs were positioned either well in front or offset to the side of the target areas, with the fighters acting as a buffer between the bombers and Iraqi fighter bases.

In the busy airspace, JTIDS proved its value. According to Sqn Ldr Reeves, 'JTIDS was a godsend. We had a theoretical limit of 100 tracks that could be displayed, but being equipped with a monochrome display, we had to use filters to make the picture workable. We always knew where the other JTIDS-equipped aircraft were – AWACS, F-15Cs, F-15Es and our tankers, although the tankers often dropped off the net just when we needed to find them. We had no onboard electronic ID capability to declare an aircraft hostile, but with JTIDS, another platform could do that for us, and this was something we trained for regularly'.

As the ground forces captured Iraqi airfields that could be used as diversions, the Tornado F 3 force was able to extend its mission length up to eight hours. This development also coincided with fewer tankers being available, as they were being tasked in support of strike packages. However, the intensive flying and long sortie lengths took a toll on the aircraft, and on occasions the operational commitment was compromised by unserviceabilities.

On the night of 5 April, only one Tornado F 3 made it to the tanker for refuelling. There, the crew found a single Tornado GR 4 whose wingman had also become unserviceable. Since singleton aircraft were not permitted to enter the AOR, it seemed that the Tornado GR 4 mission would be cancelled, but the quick-thinking Tornado F 3 crew arranged via secure radio to be re-tasked to fly as an escort for the strike aircraft. As a result, the Tornado GR 4 successfully attacked its target near Baghdad while the Tornado F 3 flew in formation, ready to warn of any SAM launches or AAA fire.

The Tornado F 3 crews had played a major part in the shaping of the battle space in the early parts of the campaign, but by April 2003 they had done their job and the Coalition air forces had achieved air supremacy. The last Tornado F 3 mission of Operation *Telic* was flown on 7 April 2003, after which the aircraft and crews were withdrawn from PSAB. Flt Lt Macintyre summed up the performance of the aircraft and crews;

'The Tornado F 3 in the Gulf War was a good bit of kit. It had come a very long way from the beast of the late 1980s/early 1990s. The radar was good [but] datalink was a real ace. The RHWR was as good as any, and the TRD was a proven defence against all the single-digit SAM systems. The airframe was still not a dogfighter, and never would be. The main missile [SuperTEMP Skyflash] was outdated, and being semi-active, it made the fighter vulnerable. This was to change over the next few years with the Stage 3 radar, supporting mid-course guidance for the AIM-120 AMRAAM. Combined with the AIM-132 ASRAAM, we finally had a seriously potent sword.'

## BALTIC AIR POLICING – OPERATION *SOLSTICE* (2004–05)

When the Baltic states of Lithuania, Estonia and Latvia joined NATO in March 2004, a NATO Air Policing capability was established at Šiauliai air base in Lithuania. The mission was to provide the new members, which did not have their own air defence forces, with the same measure of security as that enjoyed by other NATO members.

The Baltic airspace is busy with flight activity by the Russian Federation Air Force because of the Russian enclave of Kaliningrad, which sits between Lithuania and Poland. Russian military aircraft regularly fly over the sea from mainland Russia to Kaliningrad without submitting flight plans, often approaching NATO airspace without contact with air traffic control (ATC) agencies or displaying transponder codes.

On 14 October 2004, two Tornado F 3s from No 43 Sqn, led by Sqn Ldr D J Storr, arrived at Šiauliai to take over from Royal Danish Air Force F-16s. A fortnight later, two more Tornado F 3s brought the detachment up to its full strength of four aircraft. The No 43 Sqn detachment lasted for six weeks, and it was replaced in sequence by personnel from No 111 Sqn, No 11 Sqn and, finally, No 25 Sqn, who handed over to the F-16s of the Royal Norwegian Air Force in January 2005.

'We occupied a squadron HAS site in the southeast corner of the airfield', wrote Flt Lt Macintyre. 'It was quite strange to see the old Soviet HAS buildings. The Tornado aircraft were kept in two "Rubb" hangars near to the eastern threshold of the runway. They were located about 800 m from the squadron HQ, and therefore we had a coach on standby to take everyone out there if the hooter went'. The main challenge to both air- and groundcrew was the cold weather typical of the Baltic winter, where temperatures of -15°C are not uncommon. 'The days passed reasonably quickly', continued Macintyre, 'and we soon realised the chances of us doing any flying were very slim. There was no hint of any Russian or Belarus air activity during that time'. (*text continues on page 51*)

# COLOUR PLATES

**1**
Tornado GR 1 ZA470/AJ-L (Operation *Jural*), Dhahran, Saudi Arabia, 1992

**2**
Tornado GR 1 ZA452/BP (Operation *Ingleton*), Dhahran, Saudi Arabia, 1993

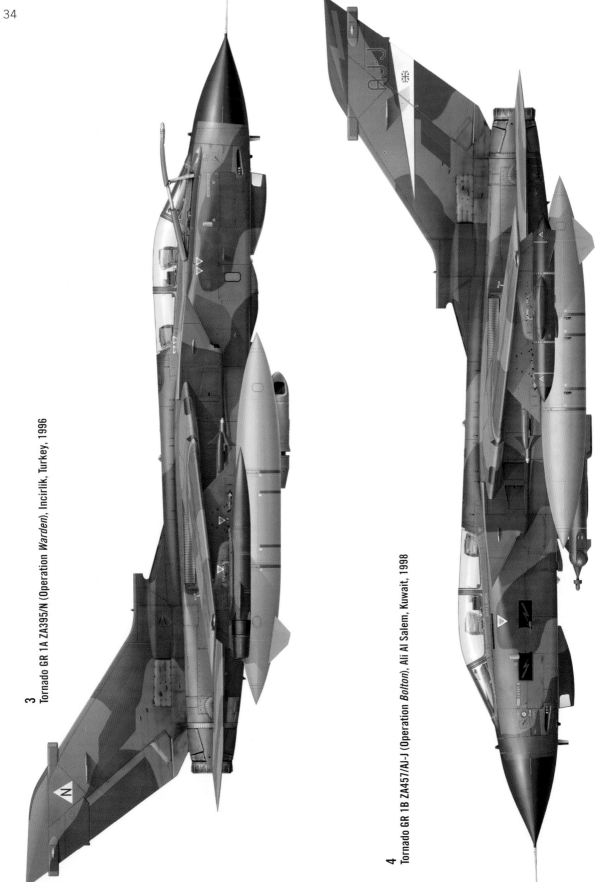

**3** Tornado GR 1A ZA395/N (Operation *Warden*), Incirlik, Turkey, 1996

**4** Tornado GR 1B ZA457/AJ-J (Operation *Bolton*), Ali Al Salem, Kuwait, 1998

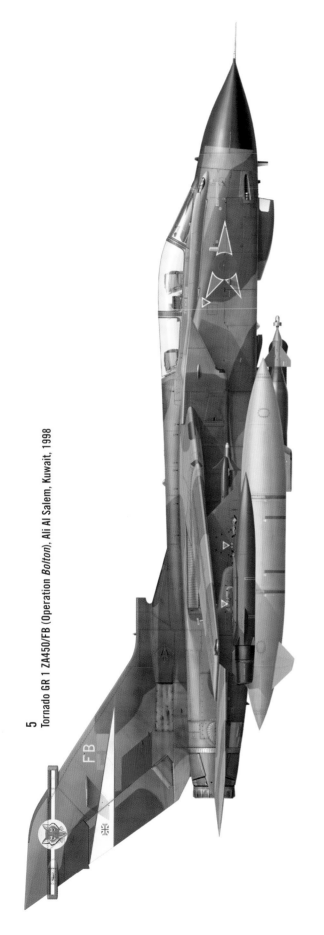

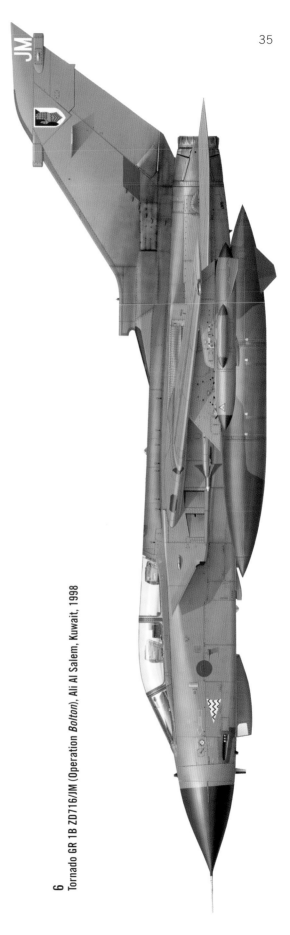

**5**
Tornado GR 1 ZA450/FB (Operation *Bolton*), Ali Al Salem, Kuwait, 1998

**6**
Tornado GR 1B ZD716/JM (Operation *Bolton*), Ali Al Salem, Kuwait, 1998

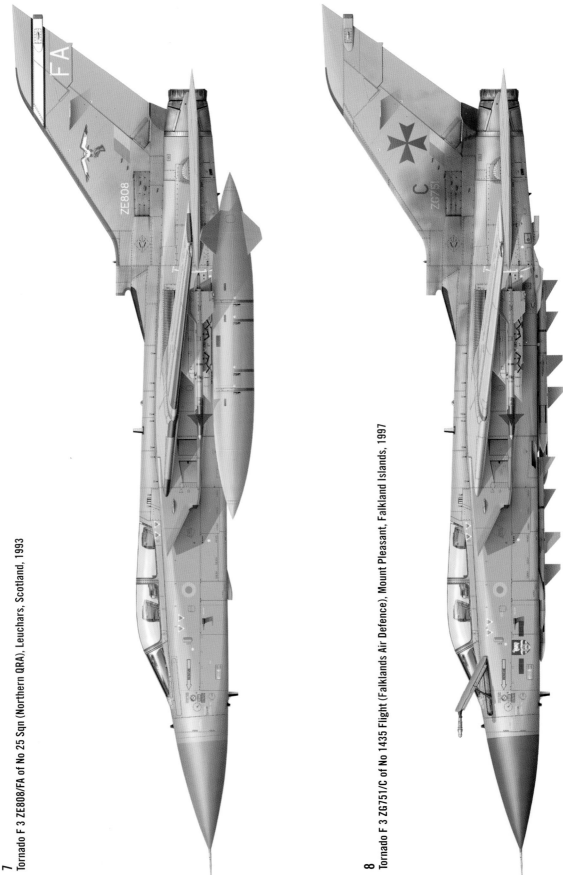

**7**
Tornado F 3 ZE808/FA of No 25 Sqn (Northern QRA), Leuchars, Scotland, 1993

**8**
Tornado F 3 ZG751/C of No 1435 Flight (Falklands Air Defence), Mount Pleasant, Falkland Islands, 1997

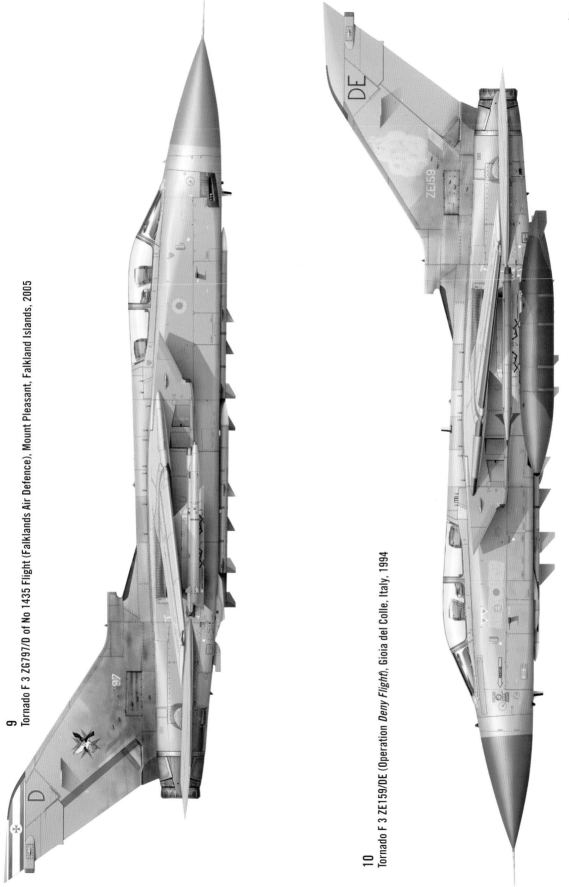

9
Tornado F 3 ZG797/D of No 1435 Flight (Falklands Air Defence), Mount Pleasant, Falkland Islands, 2005

10
Tornado F 3 ZE159/DE (Operation *Deny Flight*), Gioia del Colle, Italy, 1994

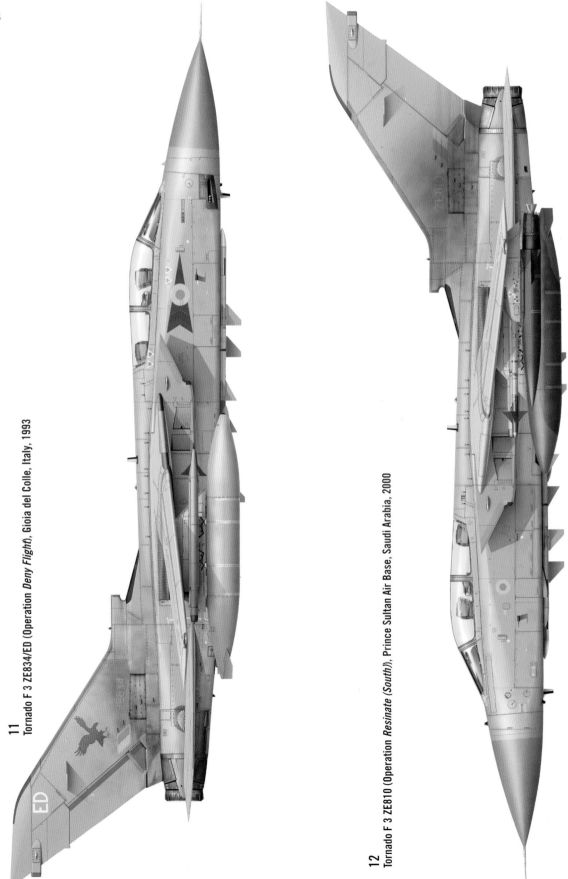

**11**
Tornado F 3 ZE834/ED (Operation *Deny Flight*), Gioia del Colle, Italy, 1993

**12**
Tornado F 3 ZE810 (Operation *Resinate (South)*), Prince Sultan Air Base, Saudi Arabia, 2000

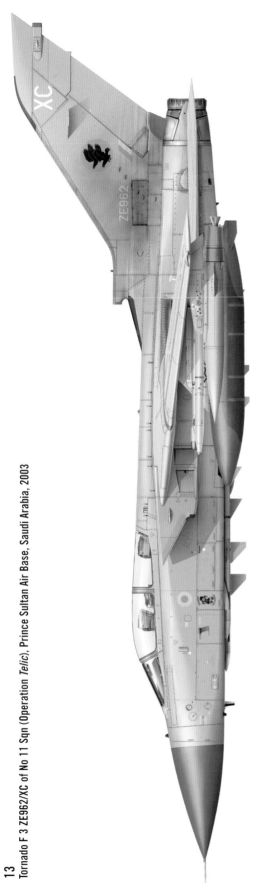

**13**
Tornado F 3 ZE962/XC of No 11 Sqn (Operation *Telic*), Prince Sultan Air Base, Saudi Arabia, 2003

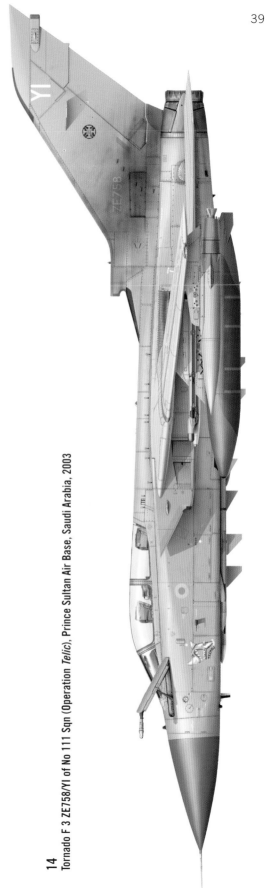

**14**
Tornado F 3 ZE758/YI of No 111 Sqn (Operation *Telic*), Prince Sultan Air Base, Saudi Arabia, 2003

**15**
Tornado F 3 ZE961/XD of No 11 Sqn (Operation *Solstice*), Šiauliai, Lithuania, 2004

**16**
Tornado GR 1 ZA470/BQ of No 14 Sqn (Operation *Engadine*), Brüggen, Germany, 1999

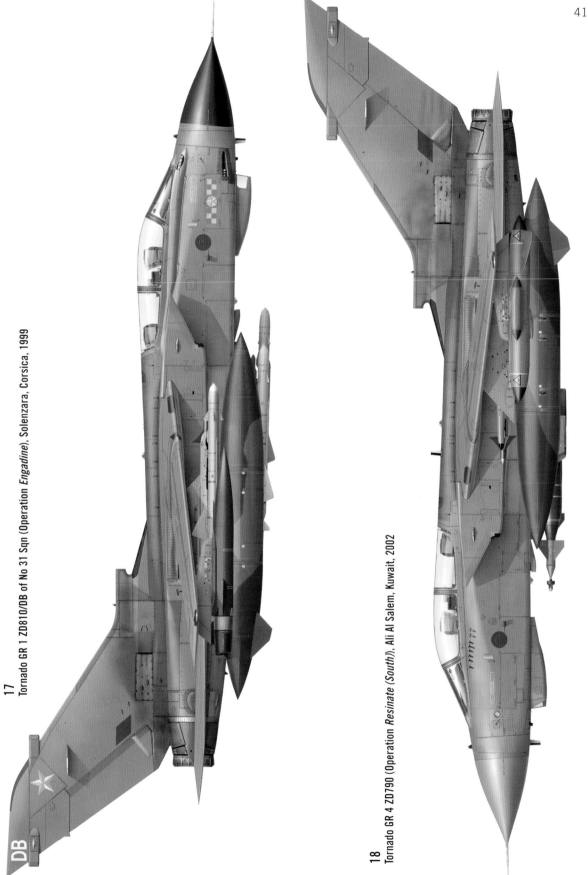

**17**
Tornado GR 1 ZD810/DB of No 31 Sqn (Operation *Engadine*), Solenzara, Corsica, 1999

**18**
Tornado GR 4 ZD790 (Operation *Resinate (South)*), Ali Al Salem, Kuwait, 2002

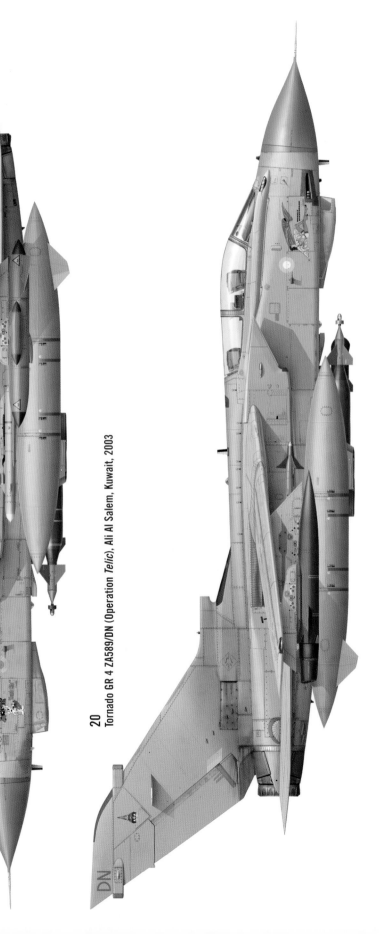

**19**
Tornado GR 4 ZA542/DM (Operation *Telic*), Al Udeid, Qatar, 2003

**20**
Tornado GR 4 ZA589/DN (Operation *Telic*), Ali Al Salem, Kuwait, 2003

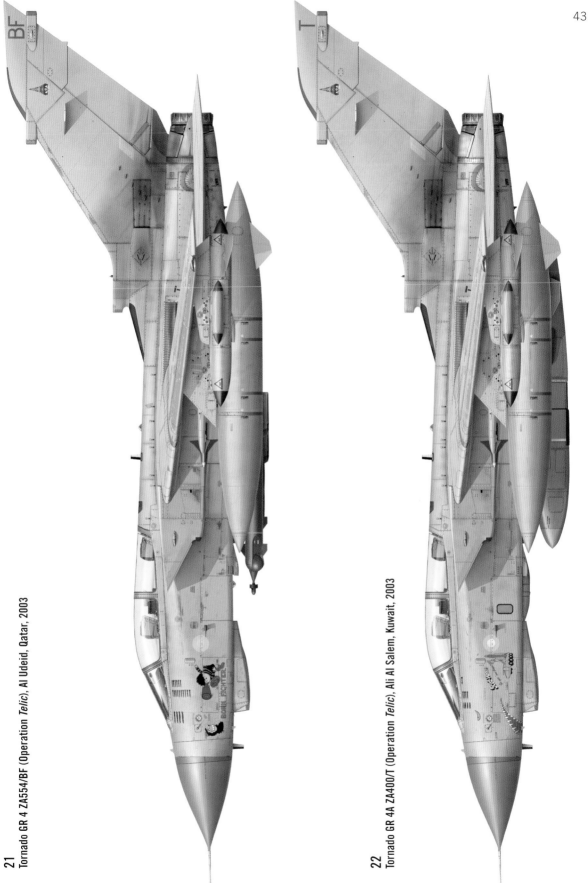

**21**
Tornado GR 4 ZA554/BF (Operation *Telic*), Al Udeid, Qatar, 2003

**22**
Tornado GR 4A ZA400/T (Operation *Telic*), Ali Al Salem, Kuwait, 2003

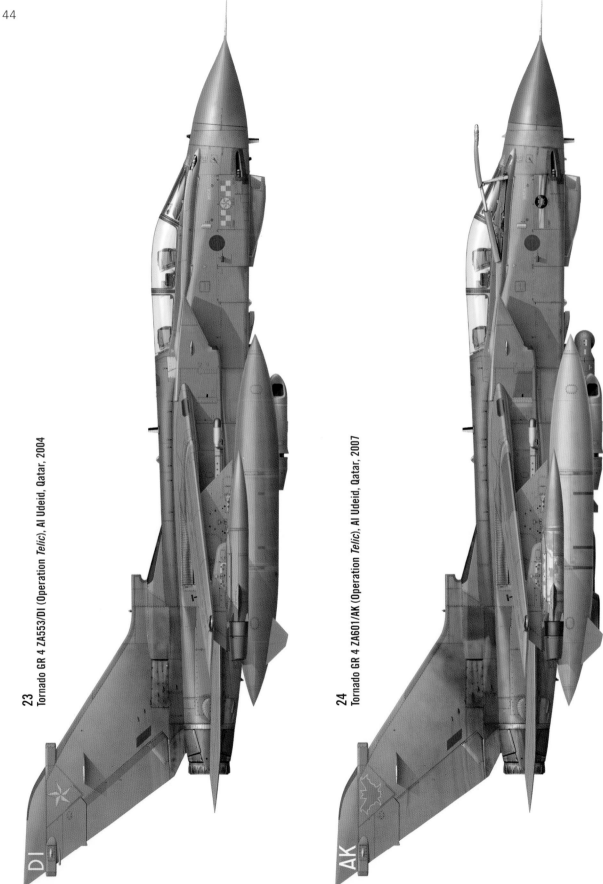

**23**
Tornado GR 4 ZA553/DI (Operation *Telic*), Al Udeid, Qatar, 2004

**24**
Tornado GR 4 ZA601/AK (Operation *Telic*), Al Udeid, Qatar, 2007

**25**
Tornado GR 4 ZA449/020 (Operation *Ellamy*), Gioia del Colle, Italy, 2011

020

**26**
Tornado GR 4 ZA553/045 (Operation *Ellamy*), Gioia del Colle, Italy, 2011

045

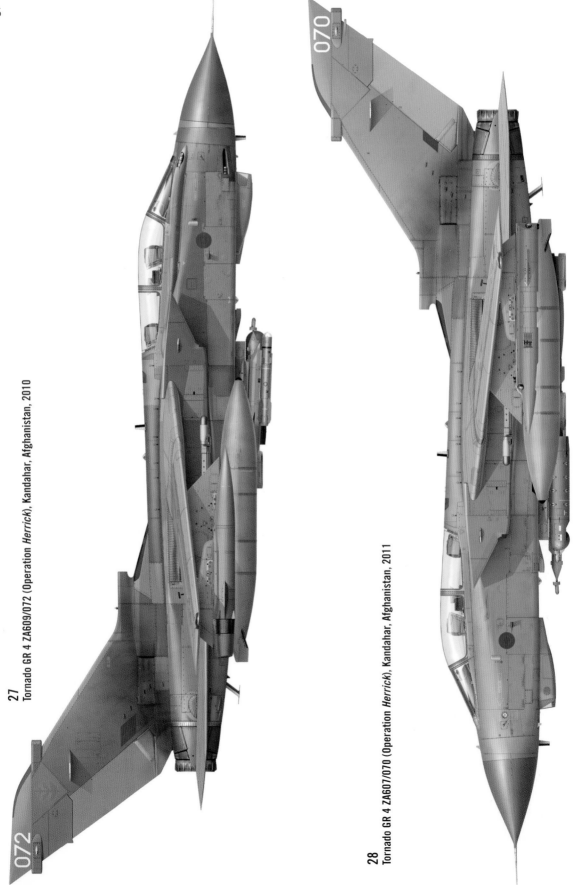

27
Tornado GR 4 ZA609/072 (Operation *Herrick*), Kandahar, Afghanistan, 2010

28
Tornado GR 4 ZA607/070 (Operation *Herrick*), Kandahar, Afghanistan, 2011

9
Tornado GR 4 ZD744/092 (Operation *Shader*), Akrotiri, Cyprus, 2018

30
Tornado GR 4 ZA543/036 (Operation *Shader*), Akrotiri, Cyprus

## UNIT BADGES

SCOTCH BROTH

FLT LT D J H MALTBY DSO DFC

FRENCH ONION

**4**
Tornado GR 1B ZA457/AJ-J of No 617 Sqn (Operation *Bolton*), Ali Al Salem, Kuwait, 1998

**5**
Tornado GR 1 ZA450/FB of No 12 Sqn (Operation *Bolton*), Ali Al Salem, Kuwait, 1998

**5**
Tornado GR 1 ZA450/FB of No 12 Sqn (Operation *Bolton*), Ali Al Salem, Kuwait, 1998

**7**
Tornado F 3 ZE808/FA No 25 Sqn (Northern QRA), Leuchars, Scotland, 1993

**8**
Tornado F 3 ZG751/C No 1435 Flight (Falklands Air Defence), Mount Pleasant, Falkland Islands, 1997

**9**
Tornado F 3 ZG797/D of No 1435 Flight (Falklands Air Defence), Mount Pleasant, Falkland Islands, 2005

**13**
Tornado F 3 ZE962/XC of No 11 Sqn (Operation *Telic*), Prince Sultan Air Base, Saudi Arabia, 2003

**13**
Tornado F 3 ZE962/XC of No 11 Sqn (Operation *Telic*), Prince Sultan Air Base, Saudi Arabia, 2003

**14**
Tornado F 3 ZE758/YI of No 111 Sqn (Operation *Telic*), Prince Sultan Air Base, Saudi Arabia, 2003

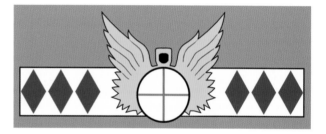

**16**
Tornado GR 1 ZA470/BQ of No 14 Sqn (Operation *Engadine*), Brüggen, Germany, 1999

**14**
Tornado F 3 ZE758/YI of No 111 Sqn (Operation *Telic*), Prince Sultan Air Base, Saudi Arabia, 2003

**17**
Tornado GR 1 ZD810/DB of No 31 Sqn (Operation *Engadine*), Solenzara, Corsica, 1999

**19**
Tornado GR 4 ZA542/DM of No 31 Sqn (Operation *Telic*), Al Udeid, Qatar, 2003

**20**
Tornado GR 4 ZA589/DN of No 31 Sqn (Operation *Telic*), Ali Al Salem, Kuwait, 2003

**20**
Tornado GR 4 ZA589/DN of No 31 Sqn (Operation *Telic*), Ali Al Salem, Kuwait, 2003

**21**
Tornado GR 4 ZA554/BF of No 14 Sqn (Operation *Telic*), Al Udeid, Qatar, 2003

**22**
Tornado GR 4A ZA400/T of No 2 Sqn (Operation *Telic*), Ali Al Salem, Kuwait, 2003

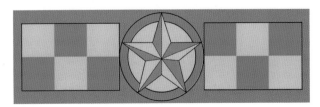

**23**
Tornado GR 4 ZA553/DI of No 31 Sqn (Operation *Telic*), Al Udeid, Qatar, 2004

**24**
Tornado GR 4 ZA601/AK of No 9 Sqn (Operation *Telic*), Al Udeid, Qatar, 2007

## CHAPTER THREE

# KOSOVO 1999

Crews from No 14 Sqn at Brüggen, commanded by Wg Cdr Timo Anderson, who participated in Operation *Engadine*. In the foreground is a 1000-lb Paveway II LGB, which was the main weapon used by the Tornado force on missions over Kosovo (*No 14 Sqn Association*)

## OPERATION *ENGADINE*

Throughout the 1990s the former Republic of Yugoslavia was riven by savage civil wars, and in late 1998 fighting broke out in nearby Kosovo. After attempts to resolve the conflict through diplomacy had failed, NATO commenced air operations against Serbia in March 1999. The RAF fixed-wing contribution to NATO forces initially comprised a detachment of Harrier GR 7s based at Gioia del Colle, which flew the first offensive sorties of Operation *Engadine* over Kosovo on 24 March 1999. Just four days later, Parliament decided to increase the number of RAF aircraft available for Operation *Engadine*, and on 28 March Brüggen's Tornados were earmarked for this commitment.

Unfortunately, No 17 Sqn had been disbanded in the week before the operation. 'We had been nominated as a "centre of excellence" for TIALD and Paveway III early in 1998 and were the lead squadron at Brüggen', remembered Wg Cdr C J Coulls, 'with No 14 Sqn nominated as next in line. My QWIs [Qualified Weapons Instructors] had become genuine experts and had actually rescued a Paveway III trial in the UK that was going badly.

'Kosovo kicked off as we were disbanding, and Paveway III was about to be used for the first time in anger – and Brüggen's experts (I still had about six crews that were TIALD/Paveway III Combat Ready) were sitting around partying. Needless to say, persuading the hierarchy to see sense and let us do the operation was not possible (I tried my hardest), so No 14 Sqn got to do it with a bunch of people that were not trained. The crews were doing the TIALD workup during the transits to the Balkans!'

As the remaining specialist TIALD/LGB unit, No 14 Sqn, commanded by Wg Cdr T M Anderson, was earmarked as the lead unit for Operation *Engadine*, and it provided 12 crews. Across the other side of the station, No 31 Sqn, commanded by Wg Cdr R A C Low, was in the final stages of its work-up for deployment for Operation *Bolton*, and it was able to provide another six crews. The remaining crews came from No 9 Sqn, commanded by Wg Cdr G J Bagwell. However, with few TIALD pods available for training outside operations in the Persian Gulf, none of the crews at Brüggen were particularly current in TIALD/LGB operations.

Photographed in a shelter at Brüggen, Flt Lts Keven Gambold (pilot) and Page (navigator) of No 14 Sqn prepare for an Operation *Engadine* mission over Kosovo in the spring of 1999 (*No 14 Sqn Association*)

A further complication was the instruction by the Air Tasking Operations Centre that Tornado missions were to be flown as six-ships, made up of two pairs of bombers each escorted by a 'spotter' to warn of SAM launches. This tactic had been adopted by the Harrier force in operations over the Balkans, and while it may have been a sensible precaution for single-seat aircraft, it was of doubtful relevance to two-seat aircraft carrying out long-range operations with laser systems. The instruction was an unfortunate example of micro-management by staff officers with little tactical appreciation, and it was to have serious consequences later both in terms of tactics and weapons accuracy.

One initiative that did work particularly well was the arrival at Brüggen during the next few days of three VC10K tankers from No 101 Sqn. A very close relationship quickly developed between tanker and Tornado crews, enabling them to operate together very effectively.

After a few days of frenetic activity at Brüggen, ten Tornado GR 1s and six TIALD pods were ready for action. Apart from preparing crews, aircraft and weapons, there was another problem to be overcome in the few days available. Although Brüggen had spent the Cold War decades at a high state of readiness for wartime operations from the station, all of that expertise had been lost since late 1989. Much of the support infrastructure had also been dismantled during the 1990s, when the emphasis had shifted to deployed operations. For example, the secure communications equipment that had been removed from the squadron operations building now had to be reinstalled.

Having made its operational debut in prototype form during Gulf War I, the GEC-Ferranti TIALD pod played a key role in Operation *Engadine* eight years later. The campaign in the Balkans quickly revealed the usefulness and limitations of the pod during sustained long-range operations in often-poor European weather conditions (*Andy Glover*)

The operational crews were divided amongst three teams – a 'green team' and a 'red team' from No 14 Sqn and a further No 31 Sqn team. The 'spotter' crews for each team were provided by No 9 Sqn.

The first operational mission from Brüggen was led by Sqn Ldrs J K Hogg and S P Rochelle on the night of 4/5 April.

Six Tornados, flown by the No 14 Sqn 'green team', were tasked against targets on the periphery of Kosovo. The first three aircraft took off from Brüggen at 2130 hrs following their VC10K tanker, with the second wave, comprising three more Tornados and another VC10K, getting airborne five minutes behind them.

No diplomatic clearance had yet been received for the operation, so instead the tankers filed a flight plan for a routine training flight to Aviano. The two formations flew southwards through eastern France to the Mediterranean coast, then routed via Corsica eastwards across Italy. There were thick clouds across France, so the Tornado pilots had to work hard to keep station with their tankers. The transit also included two refuelling brackets, which again were carried out in challenging conditions. This procedure was somewhat over-complicated by the presence of three, rather than the more usual two, Tornados with each tanker.

The aircraft broke out of the cloud as they reached the Adriatic, but the crews discovered that the whole of the airspace was already filled with other NATO tankers and strike aircraft – the Brüggen crews had not received the airspace co-ordination instructions detailing the positions of these tanker tracks! However, after being cast off by their VC10Ks, the Tornados worked their way through the mêlée and rendezvoused with pre-strike tankers to the south of Macedonia.

'This was actually a pair of TriStar tankers, operating in formation for the first time', Wg Cdr Anderson later described. 'The AAR was a nightmare – the Tornados were heavily laden and draggy with their weapons on board; the tankers were at the top of the Tornados' effective operating altitude; and the tankers, which had much more excess thrust than the Tornados, had apparently forgotten about the need to make gentle power corrections!

'I have never before or since experienced such a heart-stoppingly difficult AAR event – the Tornados were in and out of combat power just trying to get engaged, and then to stay in, all in the inky black and as the clock ran rapidly down to "push time". In the event, "Rocky" [Sqn Ldr Rochelle] made one of the ballsiest calls I've witnessed and [delayed] the whole night mission of goodness knows how many aircraft for ten minutes to enable the Tornados to tank!'

After refuelling, the Tornados crossed the border into Serbia and headed towards their targets, where they were greeted with heavy anti-aircraft fire. The first pair attacked the highway bridge at Jezgrovice (along the shores of Lake Gazivoda, 40 miles northwest of Pristina) with Paveway IIs, while the second pair delivered Paveway IIIs onto the railway tunnel near Mure (50 miles north of Pristina), on the border between Kosovo and Serbia.

The NVG-equipped spotters were able to act as pathfinders for the bomber crews. 'For example', explained Sqn Ldr D A C Legg from No 9 Sqn, 'cloud structure and gaps are clearly seen miles ahead on goggles in the dark – this allowed the spotter crews to give the best direction for an attack to the bomber crews with TIALD'.

Each bomber dropped its weapons, using its TIALD pod to self-designate. All NATO aircraft shared the same planned weapon impact time, with the objective being to achieve a simultaneous cut of all road and rail links into Kosovo. 'As our weapons impacted', recalled Sqn Ldr Rochelle, 'the whole of Kosovo lit up. There must have been 150 major

explosions around Kosovo'. After completing their attacks, the aircraft returned home via the same route, having first rendezvoused again with the TriStar tankers for post-strike AAR. The Tornados landed back at Brüggen in daylight after a seven-and-a-half-hour flight.

The following night, Flt Lt S J Hulme and Sqn Ldr A S Frost led a team from No 31 Sqn against hardened storage bunkers at Pristina airfield. 'The sortie didn't start well, with the obligatory crew-out at formation check in!', remembered Flt Lt Hulme. 'Fifteen minutes later, after a rather rapid start, and with Adrian Frost still having barely regained his composure after a bit of a sprint across the No 14 Sqn HAS site, we taxied out to chase the two VC10Ks and five Tornados that were already heading south towards the Med and the first tanker bracket off the coast of Nice.

'About halfway across France I caught up with my formation, the weather was fantastic and it made for a great sight. However, it wasn't long before I was cursing having three Tornados on each tanker as we hit the forecast poor weather off the French coast. Close formation in thick cloud, at night, on a tanker isn't fun at the best of times, but we were to get plenty of practice that first night. Kudos to the VC10K guys, as it can't have been much fun for them, especially as we all rejoined post-strike in the Adriatic with the VC10K still plugged into the back of a TriStar – and only intermittently visible as they bounced in and out of cloud. The mission went well, with good weather once we hit the "box" and target runs that went smoothly, and with only very light AAA.'

However, the remaining crews encountered problems as the unfamiliarity with laser-guided weaponry in general – and the Paveway III in particular – began to tell. 'This attack was unsuccessful as the wrong codes were given to the LGB (my first LGB sortie)', reported Flt Lt R L Hawkins, who was flying with Flt Lt T Burke. 'At that time, LGB operations were only conducted by a select few who did not wish others to know about the magic – so very few briefings were given. I typed in the correct code but did not "enter" it, so the bomb remained on the basic training setting. It missed!'

In the No 2 aircraft, Flt Lt S Oakes and Sqn Ldr J G Niven fared little better. 'My first night nerves proved to be unnecessary', declared Sqn Ldr Niven, 'as we encountered no resistance whatsoever, no AAA, no

Operation *Engadine* crews from the No 31 Sqn detachment at the *Armée de l'Air* base at Solenzara, on Corsica, pose for a photograph at the end of the campaign. Note the ALARM missile mounted on the outer stub pylon of Tornado GR 1 ZD810 (*No 14 Sqn Association*)

SAMs, no fighters. Nothing! However, the mission was almost a complete failure, with no weapons on target from our drops. The first lesson was unfolding, with the Wing's other missions producing the same result. Disappointed and relieved in equal measure, and six or so hours after taking off, we eased our way down through the dawn sky to be met by an anxious station commander. Apart from the all-important attack, all had gone like clockwork'.

Flt Lts S Reeves and I D Hendy led their 'red team' against Pristina barracks on 6 February, each bomber being armed with two Paveway IIs. 'Probably the most challenging aspect of the whole thing was the tanking on the way down during the early part', thought Flt Lt I J Cosens. 'Pretty much the whole period was stormy across southern Europe, and at our levels you spent a lot of time on the transit [in cloud] on a tanker getting bumped all over the place. It was a relief at the Adriatic to get dropped by them and go in on your own'. After leaving the tankers, the Tornados crossed into Serbia. 'There was a lot more AAA [than over Iraq]', continued Cosens, 'especially as you crossed the border. It was like fireworks night, with the tracer rounds going up much higher than I expected'.

Although NATO was operating over Kosovo virtually round-the-clock, typically mounting about 600 sorties each day, the rate of flying for Tornado crews was relatively low. With tasking for six aircraft each day, but crewing for three or four constituted six-ship formations, they might expect to fly once every three to four days.

Theoretically, the operational crews worked on a four-day cycle, commencing on the evening of Day 1 with the main mission planning, which began at 2300 hrs after the issuing of the Air Tasking Order (ATO) for the following night. During the night, the plan would be revised as the intelligence from the previous day's operations was fed back. That evening (Day 2) the crews would report for a meteorology and intelligence brief at around 2130 hrs, followed by sight of up-to-date target imagery and any final alterations to the plan, before a formation briefing at 2205 hrs.

After a final weather update, the crews would go out to the aeroplanes just after 2300 hrs to be ready for the formation check-in at midnight, with the first take-offs some ten minutes later in the early hours of Day 3. After the mission, they would stand down for a day and then start the process again on the evening of Day 4. In practice, however, the flying rate was less regular, as the weather over the Balkans affected tasking. Laser-guided weapons needed a clear line of sight between designator and target and bomb and target, so any substantial cloud in the target area would preclude Tornado operations.

On 12 April, the 'green team' attacked the ammunition storage facility at Čačak and targets on the nearby airfield at Obvra, some 70 miles south of Belgrade. Two nights later, it was the turn of the 'red team', which bombed Nis airfield. Although some hits were scored on both of these attacks, neither mission was entirely successful – a reflection both of the lack of practice because of the shortage of TIALD pods at Brüggen in the previous years and of the practical difficulties of laser-guided operations in cloudy skies.

Another mission against a military communications site at Ivanjila by the No 31 Sqn formation on 17 April illustrated the challenges facing the Tornado crews. After refuelling in cloud and turbulence that Sqn Ldr Niven described as 'easily the worst conditions I had ever flown in', the formation crossed the Adriatic. 'Thankfully, the weather then cleared', continued Niven, 'so we reformed into our two three-ship trail and headed off into "Badlands".

'We made ready for the attack: weapon package selected (two Paveway IIs) and TIALD uncaged – let's find that target and get the job done. But nothing happened. Reselect – a few flashes on the screen, but still nothing. Not a single TIALD operational, no weapons released. Three-and-a-half hours flying through the worst weather most of us had ever experienced, only to be denied by a system that was never designed to be flown at altitude, never mind in icing conditions'.

The TIALD pods had been designed for three- to four-hour operations in clear air-mass. The designers could never have foreseen that they might instead be used for numerous consecutive missions of twice that length, flown through almost continuous rainstorms. The same was true of the LGBs, which were also designed to be carried one way and then dropped. Those loaded onto the (superfluous) spotters were flying seven- to eight-hour return flights through cloud, ice and rain, before being re-loaded for use on another day. Wg Cdr Low recalled carrying out pre-flight checks on his weapons and finding that all three seeker heads were full of water, and therefore unlikely to guide.

Over the next fortnight the weather over the Balkans deteriorated further, resulting in Tornado missions being cancelled. 'Poor weather is to be expected in the Balkans during the spring, and it was to be a feature of the campaign for me', wrote Flt Lt Hulme, 'with a number of weather scrubs pre-launch, one cancellation before we had even made it out of the Brüggen control zone and two no-drops due to weather in the target area. The lack of GPS-guided munitions, the poor performance of those early generation TIALD pods and some tricky atmospheric conditions made for extremely challenging sorties – far harder than the conditions most were used to in the Middle East from the *Warden* and *Jural* deployments, where most of the crews at Brüggen had earned their spurs patrolling Iraq'.

In late April there was talk of a land invasion of Kosovo, and No 14 Sqn crews were stood down from medium-level operations and tasked instead with becoming current at Operational Low Flying to support ground forces. The plan was for No 9 Sqn to lead a forward deployment to Solenzara, on Corsica, at the end of May to continue the medium-level air campaign with No 31 Sqn, whilst No 14 Sqn prepared to support the ground war. No 14 Sqn crews flew a number of low-flying training sorties in Britain, before the plan changed again and they resumed laser operations over Serbia. On 28 April the squadron's 'green team' attacked the airfield at Podgorica, in Montenegro, just a short distance inland from the Adriatic coast.

Meanwhile, the No 31 Sqn formation had endured more frustration thanks to the continuing bad weather over Serbia and Kosovo. Their sortie on 25 April was cancelled shortly after take-off, but four nights later it seemed that the run of bad luck had ended. The weather cleared sufficiently, and the formation carried out a completely successful attack against the ammunition storage site at Valjevo, about 40 miles southwest of Belgrade. The following night the 'red team' attacked the petroleum, oil and lubricants (POL) storage facility at Vitanovac, a few miles southeast of Obvra.

At the end of April authorisation was granted for a more direct route to Serbia through the Czech Republic, Slovakia, Hungary and Croatia. This routing reduced sortie times to around five hours, and required just one pre- and one post-strike AAR bracket. The new route was used for the first time on 2 May for an attack on the airfield at Obvra. Although the name Obvra was marked on the NATO map, the airfield was more properly Ladeveci air base, home to a wing of J-22 Orao ground-attack aircraft and Gazelle attack helicopters.

For this mission, all four bombers, led by Sqn Ldr D W Gallie and Flt Lt E Fraser, were armed with two Paveway II LGBs. The first two were tasked against a hangar and the control tower, while the second pair were to bomb aircraft parked on hard-standings at the southeasterly end of the airfield. The attack 'package' also included four F-16CJ *Wild Weasels* and a pair of EA-6B Prowlers to provide defence suppression for this target, which was defended by at least three SAM sites known to be in the area.

After overflying Croatia and Bosnia and heading for Sarajevo, the formation turned onto an easterly heading for the attack. The Tornados met with heavy AAA as they approached the target area, and then, just after the first weapons impacted, two SA-3s were launched against them. The missiles were aimed at the No 2 jet of the lead pair, forcing Wg Cdr Anderson into a hard defensive manoeuvre to escape them. The *Wild Weasels* responded to the SAM launch by firing a HARM at the 'Low Blow' radar, but in the next few seconds three more SA-3s left the launchers.

Eight miles behind the first pair of bombers, the leader of the rear pair saw what was happening ahead. 'I could see the missiles going for the leader', reported Sqn Ldr Rochelle. 'We continued to prosecute our attack, and you can see on my TIALD video this SAM-3 screeching across the screen'. At this stage, an SA-3 missile guidance radar locked onto the spotter aircraft flown by Flt Lt Wood, who was forced to jettison his tanks and run out to the north. The rear pair was also on the receiving end of the SAM site. 'As we were coming off the target, there were missiles coming up behind us', continued Sqn Ldr Rochelle, 'and as we started to defend against those, one exploded not far behind our jet – so it was pretty hair-raising'.

Meanwhile, the crew of the fourth bomber found themselves in the midst of the action. Five SA-3 and two HARMs had already been fired during their target run. 'I saw one missile come after us and then explode below [the jet]', recalled Flt Lt K Gambold. After completing its attack, the aircraft was engaged by two more SA-3s, forcing Gambold to manoeuvre to break the radar lock. He lost a lot of altitude in the process, but he still found time to comment 'Busy tonight!' over the radio, to the amusement of the other crews.

However, the excitement was not quite over. Yet another SA-3 was launched from a second site, and to escape it, Gambold had to jettison his fuel tanks and perform a last-ditch break, before running out from the target area at low-level. According to Wg Cdr Anderson, 'the *Wild Weasels* later reported that they had never seen their HARM Targeting System scopes light up with so many radar emitters and target tracking radars simultaneously'.

Once clear of the Missile Engagement Zone (MEZ), the six Tornados gathered back together and made their rendezvous with the tanker in

Hungarian airspace. On the recovery to Brüggen, instead of the usual instrument approach to land, Sqn Ldr Gallie led the six Tornados in for a low-level break into the visual circuit to announce to the world that they were back from what had been the most difficult sortie thus far. BDA later showed that all four bombers had achieved direct hits on their aiming points.

After another break caused by the weather, operations resumed on 10 May with a mission flown by the green team against a storage facility at the barracks at Leskovac, some 45 miles northeast of Pristina. The following night, the No 31

Operation *Engadine* sorties involved long transits at medium-level supported by VC10K tankers of No 101 Sqn. Although this photograph depicts a Tornado GR 4 over the Persian Gulf, it nevertheless captures the atmosphere of a mission over Kosovo (*Paul Froome*)

Sqn team attacked the Barë Road Bridge at Mitrovica, and on 14 May the red team flew one of the last missions to use the longer southerly route to Serbia, in order to attack the POL storage facility at Sjenica airfield. This mission was not entirely successful, as low cloud interrupted the guidance of some weapons during the last few seconds of the attack.

On 19 May, the No 31 Sqn formation was tasked against a militia depot approximately ten miles west of Belgrade. Unfortunately, no-one in the tasking organisation thought to inform the bomber crews that their target was almost next door to the local Air Defence Operations Centre, and that it might, therefore, be keenly defended.

'The target was a small complex only a couple of hundred feet across and with four separate DPIs', recalled Flt Lt Hulme, who led the sortie. 'The combination of still wind conditions and lots of built-up areas meant I split my six-ship into two and planned a 15-minute break between attacks. It was a bit unusual, but I didn't see many other options.

'Everything went well, with a direct hit on the target, and then as we made a hard 90-degree left turn to avoid flying over Belgrade, the sky suddenly filled with AAA that appeared to be bursting around my ears. I kept the weave going as we headed back to the west, and a few seconds later, as I banked to the right, I caught site of a bright flash at ground level and then two bright orbs of light snaking upwards. My RHWR was clear, but I was taking no chances and manoeuvred aggressively until it was clear they were not tracking me.

'It wasn't until the debrief, and we had listened to all the time synchronised TIALD videos, that we worked out I had seen a salvo of SAM-3s fired at my No 3, who had a pretty close shave having not reacted to his RHWR indications until a little too late for comfort. Composure regained, and having ascertained that we had hit the first two DPIs, I made the decision to abort the second half of the formation – needless to say, there were no complaints, as they had seen the chaos unfold in the distance.'

In the No 2 aircraft, Sqn Ldr Niven commented that 'it's fair to say that my one sortie in the vicinity of Belgrade exposed me to the most spectacular firework display I will ever witness, with AAA tracer everywhere. SAMs as well, possibly, but I didn't see any too close to us. We lined up in trail, the target a storage site. Soon, our leader was calling "chaff, flares" – the action call for defensive measures to be deployed. Then "tanks" – again an action call in response to a severe and imminent threat – for the man-in-back to jettison the almost-full fuel tanks and bomb load, shedding a great deal of weight and permitting greater manoeuvrability. They were only a few minutes ahead of us, but were getting all the attention; to be honest, I was quite happy with that. You could hear the tension in Gilbert's [Flt Lt Hulme's] voice as he made the calls.

'I had a good look out around us, before going heads-in for our attack. We did have No 3 behind us, whose job was to watch our tail. It was more of a psychological boost, as quite how they would spot a missile heading our way in the gloom is anyone's guess. So we pressed on. Again, I had a very good mark on the target, followed by weapon release. There was an almighty explosion, and a fireball that blanked my screen for a time, then a pall of smoke and flame rising rapidly into the air – job done.'

Over the next week it was the turn of the Nos 9 and 31 Sqn crews to stand down from operations, as they set up the forward operating base (FOB) at Solenzara. However, the No 14 Sqn crews kept up the pressure – on 24 May, the Batanjnica petrol storage facility was attacked, as was the ammunition storage at Ralja, 30 miles southeast of Belgrade, two days later. On 27 May, the Belgrade SAM support facility was bombed, and the following day the ammunition storage sites at Boljevac, 100 miles southeast of Belgrade, and at Sremska Kamenica, near Novi Sad, were also attacked.

'Strangely enough, the further into Serbia you went, the less intense the air defence', reported Flt Lt Cosens. 'Maybe there wasn't much left of it after those early days. The first time we were given a target in the Belgrade area, surrounded by a fully integrated air defence system, we were all a little surprised by the fact it was probably the quietest night we had'. However, this was not true of Ralja on 26 May, which was particularly heavily defended. Apart from heavy AAA, Wg Cdr Anderson recorded that three SA-6s were launched during his attack.

The Boljevac/Sremska Kamenica mission on 28 May marked the end of direct operations from Brüggen. By then, the Solenzara detachment was fully operational, and the remaining Tornado operations over Serbia were mounted from there.

On 4 June, Flt Lt Hulme led his formation against a radio relay site at Rudnik, but they were unable to drop any weapons because of the weather. The next day, a formation from No 9 Sqn was also thwarted by weather, and their mission was cancelled as they waited in the AAR tracks.

The final Tornado GR 1 mission of the air campaign over Kosovo, flown on 7 June by a No 31 Sqn formation, was also the first daylight sortie carried out by RAF Tornados. Led by Flt Lt Hulme and Wg Cdr Low, the formation carried out an Air-Launched Anti-Radiation Missile (ALARM) attack on an SA-6 battery near Sjenica. Unlike the ALARM missions flown nine years previously during Gulf War I, when the missiles were loaded on pylons beneath the fuselage, on this sortie each aircraft carried the weapons on stub pylons above the underwing fuel tanks. The mission was successful, and NATO air operations formally ceased three days later. The Solenzara detachment stayed in-theatre for another two weeks, before they were recalled, returning to Brüggen on 23 June.

## CHAPTER FOUR

# IRAQ 2000–09

## OPERATION *RESINATE*

At the beginning of 1999, all flying over Iraq had been amalgamated into Operation *Resinate* – *Resinate (North)* covered the operations out of Incirlik into the northern NFZ, while *Resinate (South)* covered operations from AAS and PSAB into the southern NFZ. At PSAB, six Tornado F 3s had taken over from the Tornado GR 1 s in order to police the southern NFZ.

Although no weapons were dropped by RAF aircraft over the northern NFZ, air strikes by Tornado GR 1s (and later Tornado GR 4s) against Iraqi AAA sites and air defence units became a regular feature of operations in the southern NFZ. The Tornado F 3 crews also became accustomed to IrAF MiG-25 'Foxbats' and Mirage F1EQs attempting to dash into the NFZ to take a shot at the AWACS and *Rivet Joint* aircraft. However, the Iraqi aircraft invariably ran out of the NFZ when they were locked up by the Tornado F 3 radar.

From the end of Operation *Desert Fox* until May 2000, the Tornado GR 1s dropped the equivalent of 78 tons of ordnance over southern Iraq. This period of operations was eloquently summarised by Wg Cdr J B Klein, commanding No 14 Sqn, as 'fairly frequently bombing various relatively cheap AAA pieces with a very expensive bomb, usually under SAM and AAA fire'. The tempo of bombing sorties continued and, for example, during the No 9 Sqn operational deployment in the autumn of

Tornado GR 4 ZA453, flown by Sqn Ldr Steve Dean and Flt Lt 'Zonker' Anderson, during an Operation *Telic* sortie from Al Udeid on 10 April 2003. The aircraft is carrying two Paveway IIs and a TIALD pod beneath its fuselage. Note the empty outer stub pylons (*Kiwi Spencer*)

2000, the unit carried out an RO3 attack on a SA-3 site at Al Kut on 9 October and an RO1 attack on a S-60 battery at Basra on 2 November.

Although most of the squadrons had given up their last Tornado GR 1s in late 2000, a handful of the aircraft continued to be used for Operation *Resinate* through 2000–01. The last operational sortie flown by a Tornado GR 1 from AAS was in mid-2001, by which time a sufficient number of Tornado GR 4s had been modified to meet the operational requirements in-theatre.

Meanwhile, RAF Brüggen closed during 2001, and its flying squadrons had been redeployed to the UK. The two ALARM-specialist units, Nos 9 and 31 Sqns, had joined the two reconnaissance units at Marham, thus – in theory at least – forming a reconnaissance/SEAD wing, while the last unit to leave Brüggen, No 14 Sqn, had moved to Lossiemouth in December 2000 to join Nos 12 and 617 Sqns. The Tornado F 3 force lost another unit in 2002 when No 5 Sqn at Coningsby was disbanded.

In 2002, the Order of Battle of the RAF Tornado force was as follows:

| RAF Strike Command | | |
|---|---|---|
| No 1 Group | | |
| Marham | No 2 Sqn | Tornado GR 4 |
| | No 9 Sqn | Tornado GR 4 |
| | No 13 Sqn | Tornado GR 4 |
| | No 31 Sqn | Tornado GR 4 |
| Lossiemouth | No 12 Sqn | Tornado GR 4 |
| | No 14 Sqn | Tornado GR 4 |
| | No 617 Sqn | Tornado GR 4 |
| Leuchars | No 43 Sqn | Tornado F 3 |
| | No 111 Sqn | Tornado F 3 |
| Leeming | No 11 Sqn | Tornado F 3 |
| | No 25 Sqn | Tornado F 3 |

# OPERATION *RESINATE (SOUTH)*

In November 2002, when No 14 Sqn deployed to Kuwait to take over Operation *Resinate (South)* from No 12 Sqn, the pace of operations had quickened. During the course of the year, the UN and Iraq had moved into an impasse about Weapons of Mass Destruction and the US government had started moving towards another war with Iraq. Iraqi forces were markedly more aggressive to Coalition aircraft operating in the Southern No Fly Zone – three SAMs were launched and AAA was fired at Sqn Ldr M J Entwistle and Wg Cdr Klein on a reconnaissance sortie over Iraq on 14 November.

The Tornado GR 4 detachment at AAS now had a new reconnaissance sensor in the RAPTOR (Reconnaissance Airborne Pod for Tornado), a long-range electro-optical and infra-red sensor pod which was carried under the aircraft. RAPTOR's imagery could be transmitted by datalink in real-time to analysts on the ground, making the Tornado GR 4 an incredibly powerful reconnaissance asset for the Coalition. Unfortunately, pilots were not overly impressed with the effects of the weight and drag of the large pod on the unimpressive handling characteristics of the aircraft at medium-level.

One of the RAPTOR tasks was to try to locate the exact positions of the Iraqi SAM systems within the Baghdad 'Super-MEZ'. Flt Lts R E

Mannering and A T McGlone flew two such sorties on 27 November and 8 December, Mannering recalling that 'we tickled the "Super-MEZ" to identify the SAMs using the RAPTOR – I believe this information was passed up the chain for use by other assets. I do remember the [Headquarters] at the time being very impressed and the squadron getting a pat on the back for that one'.

Drawing on the lessons of Operation *Engadine* over Kosovo, the Enhanced Paveway II system, which used GPS guidance if there was no laser designation, had been introduced into service in 2001. No 14 Sqn crews got to use the new weapon in anger on several occasions as the unit took part in a concerted campaign against the Iraqi air defence system in the run up to an increasingly inevitable war.

On the first such strike, on 18 November, Sqn Ldr Entwistle and Wg Cdr Klein led six aircraft against the air defence operations centre at Tallil. The lead crew dropped a single 2000-lb Paveway III onto the operations bunker, while the rest of the formation attacked other targets in the complex with Enhanced Paveway III. At this stage, the latter weapon was still something of a novelty, and as Wg Cdr Klein put it, 'it was certainly unusual and out of the ordinary compared with the "normal" run of the mill drops of Enhanced Paveway II.

'On that particular sortie, the IR conditions weren't great, and TIALD didn't produce the greatest picture on the TV TAB [cockpit display unit]. The bunker just about appeared out of the murk before weapon release. Enhanced Paveway III drops were always at greater range than their smaller Enhanced Paveway II counterparts, which increased the pressures in target identification.'

Usually, a formation of six aircraft would include four bombers and two RAPTOR jets, which could transmit real-time BDA to the air tasking agency.

Paveway II-armed Tornado GR 4 ZA559 starts up at AAS for an Operation *Resinate* sortie (*No 14 Sqn Association*)

Four consecutive days of offensive missions started on 20 November with an attack by another six-ship on the cable repeater station at Al Kut. Formations of six aircraft then bombed the 'Spoon Rest' radar at Shaibah and the fibre-optic cable repeater station at Al Uzayr (to the south of Al Amarah). RAPTOR sorties were flown over Iraq for the next three weeks, but the aircraft in the RO1 hold were not called into action. Then on 14 December, Sqn Ldr W P Bohill and Wg Cdr Klein led six aircraft against a cable repeater station at Abu Zawbah, between Basrah and Al Amarah.

The next day, after refuelling from a USAF KC-10, another four-ship attacked a 'Spoon Rest' at Al Kut. The destruction of the radar with a single Enhanced Paveway II dropped by the lead aircraft stirred up a hornets' nest of AAA, so the formation was re-tasked to bomb the nearby cable repeater station in response. A third consecutive day of offensive action followed with an attack on cable repeaters at An Nasiriyah by four aircraft.

After a relatively quiet fortnight, the Tornado GR 4s were called into action again on 30 December when Sqn Ldr Bohill and Wg Cdr Klein led another formation on a night-time strike on the air defence operations centre at Al Kut. This was the last offensive action by No 14 Sqn crews before the end of their deployment. By now it was obvious that war was imminent, and that the next unit at AAS, No 31 Sqn, would see plenty of action.

# OPERATION *TELIC*

Preparations for the invasion of Iraq started in late 2002. The 12 Tornado GR 4s of No 31 Sqn at AAS were boosted by the arrival of a further six aircraft, with additional crews from Nos 2, 9, 13 and 617 Sqns. At PSAB, the Tornado F 3 detachment was reinforced by Nos 43 and 111 Sqns, bringing the numbers up to 14 aircraft. When the Turkish government refused to allow offensive operations against Iraq from their airfields, another Tornado GR 4 base was established at Al Udeid, in Qatar, with 12 aircraft and crews drawn from Nos 12, 2 and 617 Sqns.

The invasion of Iraq, codenamed Operation *Telic*, started on the night of 19 March 2003, with attacks carried out by cruise missiles and F-117s. The first Tornado GR 4 missions were flown two days later when aircraft attacked artillery positions and other military installations as far north as Al Kut with LGBs.

The attacks by Coalition aircraft, including Tornado GR 4s, in the months before the invasion had successfully dismantled much of the enemy's air defence system. Nevertheless, Coalition aircraft operating over Iraq would be met with spirited resistance from the Iraqi defences, including SA-2s and SA-3s. Once formal hostilities started, air power was concentrated against Iraqi Republican Guard units.

One of the first missions on 21 March – a SEAD wave to take down the remaining radars prior to the major push – was flown by Flt Lt A Robins of No 9 Sqn;

'Dave [Flt Lt D R Williams] and I are No 2 in a four-ship with a five-ALARM fit. Each aircraft has an AIM-9L, BOL-IR in countermeasures in the AIM-9L pylon, "big jugs" [2250-litre external tanks], BOZ and ECM, and five ALARMs – quite the load out. We push over the border on time, but just prior, Dave and I get an ESM Caption. This tells us that our aircraft is suffering from the avionics cooling problem that the GR 4 was so often afflicted by. We then start losing ancillary items, which is all fine, as they are part of the GO/NO GO matrix.

'We then lose the RHWR, which is a bit awkward, but Dave and I know that we will get plenty of warnings (for the serious kit such as SAM-6) from the Skyshadow ECM jamming pod. We elect jointly that if I fly on the boss's wing to the Baghdad target release point, we can effectively share their RHWR, split near the target to get separation for the ALARM firing and then find them again for the egress – that was the plan, anyway! I manage to fly formation on NVGs – somewhere between "fighting wing" and "arrow" – whilst maintaining some sort of lookout below for launches; bad weather makes it tricky and we have to tighten up close for cloud.

'We anticipate our release point, and with some great timing guidance from Dave, we get to our release point in the lead pair and then we get a flash from a Roland SAM just at firing point. I pull the trigger on our ALARMs – massive pause (there always is, isn't there!) and then four out of five telegraph poles hoof into the dark with a massive bang. We've got one hang-up, and we've been spotted (nothing seen coming up apart from the AAA).

'Now my pressing problem is finding the boss in the dark to get home – or I'm going to be naked. We manage to get back together relatively uneventfully as we head home. As we head into southern Iraq, all the roads appear to be filled with snaking green lines of NVG-marked dots. It takes me a while to work out that all the vehicles that have been massing in Kuwait over the last few months are already on the road. Every road into Iraq is simply rammed with the green dots – snaking lines of NVG-marked armour.'

Two pairs of Tornado GR 4s from AAS also carried out the first operational launches of the MBDA Storm Shadow stand-off missile, with weapons being used against Iraqi air defence bunkers at Taji and Tikrit. Despite firing them from a long stand-off distance, the first pair of jets, flown by Sqn Ldr A Myers, with Wg Cdr D Robertson (OC No 617 Sqn), and Sqn Ldr Knowles, with Flt Lt A Turk, were both engaged by SA-2s during their attack. In all, a total of 27 Storm Shadow missiles would be fired during the campaign.

Two missions were launched from Al Udeid that night (21 March) – firstly, an eight-ship led by Wg Cdr M Roberts (OC No 12 Sqn), and secondly, seven aircraft led by Sqn Ldr K Rumens, with Flt Lt T Carr. The target for the first mission was near Mosul, while the second mission was against the Republican Guard barracks at Saribadi, some 30 miles to the southwest of Baghdad and in the middle of the Baghdad 'Super-MEZ'.

Aiming to minimise the exposure to the defences in the target area, Rumens planned to attack from line abreast, with each aircraft firing two ALARMs before dropping their Enhanced Paveway II simultaneously onto the GPS target position.

'We took off in the dark, but as we neared Baghdad', Rumens recalled, 'the sun started to appear on the horizon. At the predetermined point, we turned into a seven-ship "wall" and launched 14 ALARMs into the air. They all accelerated and climbed. As they went through approximately 30,000 ft, they all started to produce contrails. I remember thinking to myself that it looked like a scene out of the movie *Armageddon*. Shortly afterwards the formation dropped 21 Enhanced Paveway IIs within about two seconds of each other. The Intelligence Officer would show us some satellite imagery a few days later that would confirm 21 direct hits!'

Unfortunately, on 22 March, a Tornado GR 4 of No 9 Sqn was shot down in error by a USAF Raytheon MIM-104 Patriot missile while returning to AAS from a mission, killing the crew, Flt Lts K B Main and D R Williams.

That same night, Flt Lt T J Lindsay and Flt Lt N P Bury took part in a strike from Al Udeid on the Republican Guard barracks at Saribadi. 'We were fragged as a four-ship', recalled Bury, 'with Flt Lts Howie Edwards and Gary Partridge as my element lead. The flow into Iraq was a simple system of height and direction deconflicted corridors from Kuwait, along the Saudi border, with arms leading off at various points into Iraq.

'Our task was to drop Enhanced Paveway IIs on a Republican Guard barracks on the south side of Baghdad, and on paper the transit in looked reasonably simple until you hit the "Super-MEZ" of Baghdad. Unfortunately, we were not briefed on the possible location of a SAM-3 battery, which had been reported by Intelligence but not corroborated.

'We pressed east from the Saudi border as two pairs split by about a minute, and we had not gone particularly far before all hell broke loose on the radio. Our leader was calling SAM engagements, followed by "prepare for an ejection". As the rear pair, we had seen the flare up on our NVGs, and at this point assumed that the lead pair had been shot down – a disappointing start to my first mission! As the rear element, we kicked right to sidestep the apparent threat. As it turned out, this actually directed us *into* the threat – a modified SAM-3 system. We were subsequently lit up by a SAM-3 missile guidance (MG) radar, with what appeared to be missile launches as well.

'Luckily for us, the battery had adopted the [inaccurate] technique of launching and then delaying illuminating with MG. This minimised our warning of a shot, but resulted in a reduced chance of hitting us. We reacted to the threat, with the upshot that our [element] leader elected to take us home due to a lack of fuel to complete the mission. Tankers were at a premium, so there was no scope for a top up pre- or post-target. It was at this point that we heard our [formation] leader had not actually ejected, but had been forced to divert into AAS. All in all, an exciting first sortie. It all seemed a bit tame after that!'

ASRAAM-armed Tornado F 3 ZE962 awaits its turn to refuel from a USAF KC-10 while a Paveway II-armed Tornado GR 4 tops up before heading for Iraq. A US Navy F/A-18C Hornet from VFA-27, embarked on USS *Kitty Hawk* (CV-63), is holding station off the tanker's port wing (*Kenneth Reeves*)

In the west of the region, Tornado GR 4s equipped with the RAPTOR pod and Tornado GR 4As with their specialist low-level reconnaissance capability were part of a force committed to hunting Scud missile launchers in the Western Desert.

A few days into the war, the tasking for Tornado GR 4s changed to Kill-box Interdiction Close Air Support (KICAS) – a US Marine Corps concept whereby Iraq was divided up into discrete 'kill-boxes'. If aircraft were tasked into an 'open' kill-box, they could attack any targets such as fielded forces and military vehicles found in the area. If it was a 'closed' kill-box, the crew would be controlled by a Forward Air Controller (FAC) onto specific targets, but as Flt Lt Bury explained, 'the limiting factor for success was nearly always communications. Finding the correct frequencies to contact the relevant E-3 for tasking, or subsequently to talk to a FAC, meant that engagement opportunities in the areas we were tasked to were scant.

'KICAS provided a much more target-rich environment. The whole of the airspace was split into 30 x 30 nautical mile boxes – kill-boxes – which had an alpha-numeric identifier and associated frequencies. As long as you were tasked to a given kill-box, and it was designated as open, you could employ weapons against the cleared target sets (armour, military equipment etc.). Often, there was a handover of targets between formations if you arrived to find a callsign working your kill-box already. Once "Winchester" [all weapons expended], the jets already in the kill-box would assume the SCAR [Strike Coordination and Reconnaissance] commander role and hand over any unserviced targets.'

These missions were flown both day and night, including a six-hour night sortie on 26 March. The previous night, a CAS mission was curtailed due to heavy electrical storms.

On 29 March, a pair of Tornados dropped two Enhanced Paveway IIs and four RBL755 cluster bombs on buildings and armoured vehicles within the Republican Guard barracks at Shaykh Mazhar, to the southeast of Baghdad. A kill-box sortie the next evening was frustrated by poor weather over the target areas and by difficulty with communications.

By the beginning of April, US troops were approaching the outskirts of Baghdad, and on the 4th, US Army infantry units captured Saddam International Airport. Flt Lts Lindsay and Bury were involved in this action, dropping two Enhanced Paveway IIs on tanks that were firing on US forces. More kill-box sorties were flown over the next ten days to the north of Baghdad, including one mission on the night of 9 April when vehicles and artillery in berms were engaged with three Enhanced Paveway IIs. Two days later, a pair of Tornado GR 4s destroyed an SA-2 system near Tikrit. On his last sortie over Iraq on 14 April, Flt Lt Bury located missiles mounted on trucks to the north of Baghdad but was unable to get clearance to attack them. However, by then the land war was virtually over.

'The US troops wanted full control of all entry and exit points around Baghdad', recounted Sqn Ldr Rumens. 'To that end, we dropped all but two bridges into and out of Baghdad. The FACs would actually walk onto the bridge with handheld GPSs. They would read us the co-ordinates and then we would use Enhanced Paveway II bombs, often dropping through cloud. We could use the TIALD and laser the bombs in if there was no cloud, or if we had doubts about the GPS co-ordinates. Target Location

A line up of DJRP-equipped Tornado GR 4s at AAS in late 2003, reflecting the emphasis on reconnaissance work immediately after Operation *Telic* had ended. The aircraft (with ZA560 in the foreground) still wear artwork and bomb tallies that were applied during the conflict (*No 14 Sqn Association*)

Error [TLE] was a problem when bombing GPS-only. However, the man on the ground with a handheld GPS took the TLE problem away'.

After the war in Iraq, a significant British Army presence remained in the south of the country. A detachment of between six and eight Tornado GR 4s provided CAS for ground troops, but the Tornado F 3s were stood down from operations over Iraq.

Returning to Kuwait in August 2003, Flt Lt P D Froome of No 14 Sqn felt that 'there was a much more relaxed feel to the detachment in terms of tension with the medium-level threat removed, although there was risk on approach if you diverted in-country. The tempo was still there though with the sheer amount of recce tasking. This detachment was entirely recce – every jet with a DJRP [Digital Joint Reconnaissance Pod – broadly similar to the Vicon pod that had been used previously], every sortie involving recce of some description, as well as route searches/show of presence. The Main Supply Routes were divided up across Iraq, and time and direction allocated to avoid nasty encounters. The guns were loaded though in case you were called on to support a ground callsign'.

The daily reconnaissance flights were flown in pairs, with both aircraft fitted with a DJRP. Since there was no air-to-air threat, the Tornados no longer carried AIM-9Ls, and the original LAU-7 pylons were replaced with BOL rails. From AAS, the Tornados ranged all over Iraq and covered all the borders.

With the immediate threat from Iraq removed, the Kuwaitis were keen to reclaim AAS for themselves, and the RAF was informed that the airfield would be closed to its aircraft, ostensibly for runway resurfacing, from the end of August. For the rest of Operation *Telic*, the Tornados would operate from Al Udeid, just to the southwest of Doha. The move there was made on 25 August. According to Flt Lt Froome, 'we completed the move without any break in operational tasking, and actually flew the jets down off the back of op sorties. We had six aircraft deployed, and we flew three pairs that day. I led one pair with Colin Basnett [OC No 14 Sqn]. We were the last pair to leave AAS, and joined up with the previous pair after tasking to arrive at Al Udeid as a four-ship'.

Although the new base was comfortable enough, it was an hour's transit time to and from the Iraqi border, so operational sorties would require AAR support and would last considerably longer than had been the case from Kuwait. The main source of AAR support was a VC10K tanker, but other tankers such as USAF KC-10s and KC-135s were also used. Flt Lt Froome spent many hours 'photographing pretty much all of the borders of Iraq during that detachment. The sorties were mostly five hours long, and involved at least two tanking brackets'.

By 2004, the situation in Iraq had changed. The insurgency had started, and as Flt Lt Froome put it, they were 'supporting the guys on the ground in a more direct manner, flying in pairs. This meant that one jet would have the recce pod and the other would have the bomb and TIALD pod. We ended up split into a day and night shift, and there was careful management of who flew because we all rapidly approached the 90 hours per month limit.

'When the US Marine Corps surged into Fallujah, the British Army moved up to cover the resulting gap to the south of Baghdad. We spent a lot of the night tasking in early November covering that move north, and subsequent operations. Later November sorties were further north than Baghdad.'

Most missions lasted in excess of six hours, and despite the interesting developments on the ground, the flying was usually rather mundane in nature.

For Flt Lt Froome on the night shift there were 'surges of adrenaline for the tanking', but little else of interest. However, the day shift seemed to have a more exciting time. On 13 October, Flt Lt Kidd and Sqn Ldr D J A Potter responded to a Troops In Contact (TIC) incident during an eight-hour sortie and delivered two Enhanced Paveway IIs on an arms dump being used by insurgents. On 3 November Sqn Ldr J N Tiddy and Flt Lt A D Glover were leading a pair of aircraft on a pipeline search over northwest Iraq. The sortie profile included training for a Joint Terminal Air Controller (JTAC), but they were also called upon to provide a Show of Force (SOF) to support Coalition troops.

'We were flying airborne CAS as a pair for a team of US JTACs when they reported a large group of people moving towards their position', recalled Flt Lt Glover. 'At that time, conducting an SOF was a fairly commonly used tactic. One aircraft would perform the low-level SOF, while the other aircraft remained high to provide cover looking out for [missile] launches and gun fire. Following our 550-knot low-level pass directly overhead, with live Enhanced Paveway IIs clearly visible, the group seemed to lose interest in the US JTACs and dispersed!' Six days later, Sqn Ldr Tiddy and Flt Lt Glover were called in for another SOF during a seven-hour CAS sortie over northwest Iraq that included three AAR brackets.

Military activity in Iraq peaked during the insurgency of 2004–07, but the flying task remained relatively mundane during that time. When No 14 Sqn deployed to Al Udeid in January 2007, it was the first unit to use the Northrop/Rafael Litening III targeting pod, which replaced the TIALD pod operationally. The newer pod provided much better resolution that its predecessor – a capability which was badly needed in the urban environment where much of the insurgent activity was occurring. The situation in Iraq had deteriorated significantly in the previous 12 months, and the new pod soon came into its own.

An impressive head-on view at Al Udeid of a Tornado GR 4 carrying a typical post-Operation *Telic* load – a Litening III pod hangs from one shoulder pylon and a Paveway II from the other (*No 14 Sqn Association*)

Flt Lt E B Williams described how 'a typical sortie lasted between seven to eight hours in duration, with three AAR brackets. We would transit from Al Udeid up into Iraq, where our tasking would typically be in or around the Baghdad area, although missions in support of ground operation elsewhere, such as in support of UK forces in Basrah, were not uncommon.

'The flexibility offered by a pair of GR 4s meant that we would often end up working as single aircraft on different taskings – typically in support of Coalition convoys, armed overwatch of a specific area or to support a TIC. The latter would involve an immediate re-tasking in support. The FAC could request a SOF (often specifically requesting a Tornado), which involved a low-level pass (100-200 ft) at something like 550+ knots. This technique was a very effective way to disperse crowds around any hostile situation. If the situation required further involvement, then the GR 4 would typically be armed with the Enhanced Paveway II and the 27 mm gun for strafe attacks.

'The feedback we received from the FACs within theatre was very positive, and the quality of the pictures delivered by our new capability was the best from any fast air asset. This fact, coupled with the flexibility that we offered, meant that we found ourselves in situations where we would have never previously been utilised with the TIALD pod.'

In fact, on just the second day of Litening III operations, Wg Cdr Frost was asked by the FAC, 'Hey, what pod have you guys got there? You are by far the best in-theatre. I'm going to request Tornados for all sorties from now on!' Unfortunately, however, there were still not enough of the new pods to go around, so some sorties were still flown using TIALD.

'This was particularly frustrating on 28 January 2007', recalled Flt Lt Boardman, 'when I was flying in the vicinity of Baghdad with Flt Lt D Yeoman and we were called to a TIC that was developing someway to the southwest. On arrival we heard a single F-16 being cleared to conduct a strafing run against a building, having expended all of his bombs already! Taking over from the "Winchester" F-16 as second on the scene, we had a paltry load of one Paveway II 1000-lb bomb, the aforementioned TIALD pod to guide it, and about 100 rounds of 27 mm High Explosive shells.

'We were given a very brief update on the situation from an extremely distraught and obviously petrified ground commander who was in a Humvee positioned in a walled compound to the south of a fairly large village. He said something along the lines of "the entire village has been overrun by insurgents and anything to the north of my position is hostile – I need you to clear the village!" He could see a hostile "bongo" pick-up truck approaching his Humvee and asked us to take this out with our bomb as a matter of some urgency. Having located it on the TIALD pod, Dan said he was captured and, having positioned the aircraft on an attack run, I made the armament switches live.

'Just about a second before I was about to "commit" the bomb from the aircraft Dan rather animatedly told me to "Stop. Stop. Stop." as he had seen two AH-64 Apaches fly through his screen over the vehicle we were about to bomb. Rightly worried about blowing up friendly aircraft, he quickly asked if the FAC had control of the rotary aircraft in the area, and he answered in the affirmative. We therefore immediately set-up for another bombing run on the pick-up truck when the same thing happened again.

'On our third attempt, with the insurgents getting ever closer to the FAC, the pick-up truck entered a small set of trees and disappeared from Dan's TIALD display. Rather frustratingly, he would have easily been able to track the vehicle and deliver our bomb onto the target had we been carrying the new Litening III pod. Very soon after this, two "Sandy" (specially trained in the On-Scene-Commander role) A-10 aircraft arrived on scene, and, having many advantages over our single TIALD-equipped Tornado (a Sniper Pod, more fuel, many more weapons and a phenomenally powerful cannon to name but a few), we departed the area to get some more fuel and continue our briefed tasking to the north.'

A Paveway II-armed Tornado GR 4 of No 12 Sqn undertakes an operational mission over southern Iraq in November 2004 (*Andy Glover*)

This major action, which was later called the Battle of Najaf, was eventually brought to an end by American reinforcements, but not before one of the Apaches had been shot down by the insurgents.

By 2008, it was clear that the Iraqi government had gained the upper hand and that the British forces would not be needed for much longer. No 12 Sqn handed over responsibility for Operation *Telic* to No 14 Sqn in March 2008. This coincided with the start of Operation *Knight's Charge*, an Iraqi Army offensive to reclaim Basra from the militias who had largely wrested control of the city from the British Army. Many of the unit's sorties were flown in direct support of this operation, providing CAS and tactical reconnaissance for Iraqi Army units.

The challenge for the crews involved was to stay alert to what was happening on the ground while they were on station overhead for four, five or six hours at a time. Most sorties were flown as pairs, with the Tornados carrying a Litening III pod and Enhanced Paveway II, although for some missions the RAPTOR or the DJRP might be carried. As previously, the sorties started with a transit northward past Bahrain and Kuwait to the tanker towlines on the Iraqi border south of Basra. From here, the Tornados would continue to the operating area, which would usually be around Basra, but tasking as far away as Baghdad or even Kirkuk was not unknown.

The nature of the mission meant that Tornado crews had to be adaptable – CAS work over urban areas was difficult, and it was often hard to locate targets. Sqn Ldr I A Davis described a sortie with Flt Lt Williams over Basra on 1 April;

'A UAV [operator] had identified a rocket pointing at Basra air base, and he was trying to get someone to bomb it before it went off. The co-ordinates he generated were in error by up to 300 m, and a Predator UAV and a US Apache helicopter were attempting, unsuccessfully, to get "eyes on" the target. We orbited several times over the area, and it was clear that the other assets were the main focal point for the JTAC, but as we orbited, Sam highlighted a linear feature that, when we looked closer, could well have been a rocket. We told the FAC, and after a short confirmatory talk-on, he was happy we had the rocket.

'He quickly cleared the other assets out of the area and authorised our attack, with all the details, including our updated co-ordinates, which was amusing as he had to get the co-ordinates from us to then pass them back to us to make the attack legal. The target was on the edge of the "Shia flats", and when I requested the line of attack for the strike, the FAC was happy for us to nominate our own. We went to 20 miles from the target and spun round. There was a massive thump as the Enhanced Paveway II sailed off in the direction of the sand below. A few seconds later, Sam made every navigator's favourite call – "Splash". The bomb worked according to Raytheon's promotional manual and hit the target spot on. There was an almighty explosion.'

By April, the Iraqi Army had cleared most of Basra and was pushing through the northerly outskirts of Al Latif. On 4 April, Sqn Ldr Davis and Flt Lt T J B Dugan of No 14 Sqn were tasked to perform a sweep along a route to ensure that it was clear of suspicious activity before it was used by an Iraqi Army convoy. Starting at one end of the road, which ran just to the west of Al Latif, Davis and Dugan began to search its length, looking for anything that seemed out of place. Not far along the route, Flt Lt Dugan found a man acting suspiciously near a small building. Sqn Ldr Davis kept the Tornado overhead while Flt Lt Dugan monitored this unusual individual over the next few minutes as he walked to a culvert under the road, from which two others appeared. Sqn Ldr Davis watched the unfolding events from the front cockpit;

'All of a sudden, someone appeared from the outlet pipe, which got our interest. Initially, we thought they may be trying to plant an IED [Improvised Explosive Device] under the road. Within five minutes, another bloke appeared walking down the road and chatting with the three existing personnel. This got more suspicious when a car pulled up and all the personnel climbed in and drove off.'

By now the Tornado was running short of fuel, but Sqn Ldr Davis declared that 'we weren't going to leave this vehicle until we had to. Our luck was in; the hostiles drove about 800 m and then reversed up to a cross-road'. Here, two more men joined the group. Dugan tracked the suspected terrorists as they started to walk to various discrete points in the open area beyond the road, apparently retrieving items. The Litening III pod enabled him to copy down the exact co-ordinates of each of the locations that were visited.

As fuel became critical, a Predator UAV relieved the Tornado, and at the same time an Iraqi Army patrol arrived on the scene. With the help of the Litening III pod and the co-ordinates that Dugan had copied down, the crew was able to help the Iraqi Army unit carry out an effective search. Shortly thereafter, the FAC reported that they had found a major weapons cache. Hidden in the ground near to the road were a heavy machine gun with 20 boxes of ammunition, 17 50 mm mortars and 20 82 mm mortars.

After a period of nearly 20 years in which Iraq had dominated the operational life of the RAF, British operations in the country wound down in early 2009. The last Tornado GR 4 mission over Iraq was flown by a No 13 Sqn crew in May 2009.

## CHAPTER FIVE

# AFGHANISTAN AND LIBYA 2009–14

## OPERATION *HERRICK*

The release of the Tornado GR 4 from Iraq meant that these aircraft could then be deployed to Afghanistan to replace the Harrier GR 9s on Operation *Herrick*. Eight Tornado GR 4s from No 12 Sqn left Lossiemouth on 14 June 2009 to join the No 904 Expeditionary Air Wing (EAW) at Kandahar. They reached Afghanistan two days later after a night-stop at Akrotiri, and flew their first operational sortie on 24 June.

'When the Tornado force arrived', recalled Sqn Ldr F J MacDonald of No 14 Sqn, 'we in-briefed to the theatre and started flying almost straight away. I was crewed with Charlie Butterfield [Flt Lt C Butterfield]. We crewed up with a No 12 Sqn crew and flew as a dedicated pair, which meant eating, sleeping (same four-man room) and working together. This worked really well.

'The flying task was interesting and busy. CAS stacks ended up being just that, and without datalink to see the other players in the area, it was sometimes a little unnerving as an unexpected player shot through our allotted airspace – Reaper UAVs and helicopters below us, F-16s and B-1Bs above us, all itching to get involved. I remember seeing an awful lot of

Reheat leaves a shimmering haze as a Tornado takes off from Kandahar at the start of an Operation *Herrick* sortie. Reheat doubled the power of the RB199 engines in the aircraft (*Chris Stradling*)

burning armoured personnel carriers [APCs] at the TICs we were called to – it was quite depressing, and there was often nothing we could do to help.'

For missions over Afghanistan, the aircraft were configured with the Litening III targeting pod and were armed with the new Paveway IV 500 lb LGB and the DMS Brimstone missile. With their smaller warheads and their consequent lower footprint of collateral damage, both of these weapons were better suited to counter-insurgency operations than the previous generation of ordnance used in Iraq.

Operation *Herrick* marked a fundamental change in the employment of the Tornado. From the early days of the Cold War through Gulf War I, the subsequent operations in Iraq and the Kosovo campaign, the jet had been used in the interdiction role as part of larger packages of aircraft on pre-planned missions. These multi-aircraft Combined Air Operations were usually independent of ground operations, with a clear demarcation between ground and air forces. Even during the later phases of Operation *Telic*, the aircraft were launched on a pre-planned route, and although they would generally work with a JTAC or FAC, the air operations were not fully integrated into the land campaign.

In Afghanistan all that changed, with routine operations switching from the pre-planned interdiction flying of the previous 25 years to a much more fluid CAS role, where there was no 'line on the map' at the start of the sortie. Crews had to understand what was happening on the ground, and also had to know how to interpret the RoE in complex and dynamic situations.

Much of the work of the Tornado detachment was in western Kandahar Province, only a few miles away from Kandahar City, where the Taliban was pressing International Security and Stabilisation Force (ISAF) troops and attempting to extend its control. Most sorties were in direct support of ground patrols, frequently providing armed overwatch for troops engaged by Taliban groups. Crews were also routinely re-tasked to cover ISAF convoys that had been involved in roadside IED incidents.

Often, a Show of Presence flypast would deter the enemy, but if necessary, this tactic could be escalated into the more intimidating SOF and, ultimately, the use of weapons, known colloquially as 'going kinetic'. Traditional reconnaissance sorties were also routinely flown using the RAPTOR pod. Most missions were supported by AAR, often from KC-10 and KC-135 tankers, giving typical sortie lengths of between three and five hours.

Apart from the flying task, the Tornado detachment also mounted Ground-based CAS (GCAS), which involved the crews sitting at readiness awaiting the order to scramble if emergency air support was needed at short notice. Flt Lt C Stradling reckoned that 'a good average was about 15 minutes from the phone call to getting airborne (with a requirement to be airborne in less than 30 minutes). I think our first scramble was about 13 minutes'.

Flt Lt Stradling led the detachment's first operational GCAS scramble on 29 June to respond to two TIC incidents involving the Dutch contingent. During the sortie, they carried out an SOF over enemy positions near Tarin Kowt, some 70 miles north of Kandahar in Uruzgan Province. The low pass proved enough to break the contact. This province was actually in the area of responsibility of Australian forces, illustrating that although the British Army's operations were largely confined to Helmand Province, RAF aircraft were tasked over a much wider area.

Stradling completed his 4000th Tornado flying hour the following day while leading a CAS sortie firstly over Kuhak, some 95 miles south of Heart, and then Nad-e-Ali, near Lashkar Gah in Helmand Province. On 8 July the crew was scrambled from GCAS again as the No 2 in a pair to support a TIC at Shamaz, near Gereshk, about 70 miles west of Kandahar.

Flying almost daily sorties meant that crews soon racked up the hours, and 40 or 50 hours a month were usual on operations. Missions continued in the hours of darkness, and on the night of 31 July, a crew was called in to support a TIC in a semi-rural area some 60 miles northwest of Kandahar. The navigator involved described the unfolding action as 'a night drop against a group of two or three insurgents who were hiding behind a compound wall, having previously been [firing] against friendly forces in the Kajaki area. We had previously been supporting a group of British forces on a night task, and were called off to go and assist with a possible TIC. We were given confirmation of the position by a B-1B, and then set up for the attack.

'It took about 20 minutes for us to get permission to drop so close to a compound, but once it was received, we dropped a single Paveway IV against the position. On completion of the task, we returned to the previous task before flying back to KAF [Kandahar airfield], with a sortie duration of about five hours'.

Over the next three weeks, the crew flew a variety of daylight missions, including RAPTOR, CAS and GCAS sorties, which took them over much of Kandahar Province, as well as Helmand to the west.

In August two more Tornado GR 4s were added to the detachment in Kandahar, bringing the total to ten aircraft, in readiness for increased tasking during the Afghan national elections. During a sortie on 20 August, one crew intervened in two TICs, carrying out two strafing attacks on enemy positions near Sangin, where insurgents were using the cover of a hedgerow to fire upon ISAF troops.

'20 August 2009 was election day, and one of the busiest sorties I have ever flown in a Tornado', reported a navigator. 'We were sent to a number of different tasks as TICs developed and closed with amazing speed. The last event of the sortie was to support a TIC near Sangin, where the Brits had taken casualties earlier in the day, and they were again taking incoming fire from an unknown position. We did two high-angle (about 30 degree) strafe attacks against small, wooded areas close to a friendly Patrol Base. Our No 2 also did three attacks against similar positions in the hope of flushing them out, although nothing was seen. We were extremely low on fuel when we eventually handed over to a pair of A-10s.'

Flt Lt R J Boardman, crewed with Sqn Ldr P Abbott, arrived in September, and he recalled that they 'flew 30 missions on Operation *Herrick*, all bar three being at night. We soon found that the sorties were remarkably similar to those we had flown over Iraq on Operation *Telic*, without the lengthy transit at the start and end of each sortie. Indeed, instead of spending nearly an hour-and-a-half transiting up the Northern Arabian Gulf and then refuelling, you could get your tasking

This close-up view of the underside of Tornado GR 4 ZA559 shows the RAPTOR reconnaissance pod to good effect. The aircraft is also armed with a pair of Paveway IV LGBs in case it is called upon to support ground forces (*Chris Stradling*)

on the ground prior to take-off at Kandahar and be "on-task" a couple of minutes after that'.

No 31 Sqn took over the detachment in October 2009, handing over to No 9 Sqn four months later. Operation *Moshtarak*, which aimed to wrest control of the town of Marja, southwest of Lashkar Gar in Helmand Province, from the Taliban, started on 13 February 2010. The initial troop insertion was carried out by four Chinooks, which delivered more than 600 soldiers into Taliban-held territory in just over two hours.

Over the next few days, Tornado GR 4s carried out overwatch of the operation, using their Litening III pods to assist troops on the ground to locate groups of insurgents. The pods also allowed crews to track and follow suspicious persons or vehicles, often for prolonged periods of time, and to guide friendly forces to intercept them, or to engage them using Paveway IV or DMS Brimstone. On at least two occasions, No 9 Sqn crews also alerted ground forces to people digging holes near to tracks in order to plant IEDs.

During the course of 2010, No 904 EAW was manned sequentially by personnel from Nos 2 and 13 Sqns. In the summer, ISAF launched Operation *Hamkari* to take back western Kandahar from the Taliban. This fertile region, extending some 30 miles westward from Kandahar City itself, lies on either side of the Arghandab River and is bounded in the south by the Dowry River (with desert beyond) and to the north (with mountains beyond) by Highway 1, the main road between Kandahar and Herat.

Heavy vegetation gave some cover from aerial surveillance, while the maze of compounds and villages in the area made it ideally suited for the Taliban to convert into strongpoints and IED factories. They also defended the area with extensive IED belts and booby-traps. From this secure base, the Taliban was able to control much of the region, including most of Highway 1.

When No 2 Sqn crews returned to Marham at the end of July, they had flown approximately 500 operational sorties, of which around a fifth were GCAS scrambles. A No 2 Sqn pilot described one such mission;

'Get to the jets, heart racing, the "auth" [Authorising Officer – the officer at Kandahar running the operations desk and managing the flying programme] tells us we are off to a kill-box 300 miles away right up in the northwest corner, Spanish TIC. Everything stops at Kandahar, GCAS has priority, airborne within 13 minutes of the horn blasting. Park the throttles top left-hand corner. Forty miles out and we get contact with the Spanish JTAC. He sounds pretty cool, and he gives us a situation update – a foot patrol on the ground is taking effective fire from nearby compounds. Unable to locate accurate enemy firing points, an SOF is in order. Here we go, quick chat with the navigator, our turn for the show, with my wingman sitting high watching our tail.

'I drop the nose, and in a flash we are at around 130 ft, 550 knots, hoovering along. The shock and awe will do it, and it is usually enough to break the contact as the enemy knows what comes next. We pull up and sit with our wingman in the overhead, ready for further words from the JTAC. After 20 minutes or so he is happy, and clears us to the tanker.'

When No 14 Sqn deployed to Afghanistan in the autumn of 2010, much of the tasking was still in support of Operation *Hamkari*. On 11 October, Canadian exchange officer Capt J J Janjua flew his first sortie, and it took him over Panjwai, where, by coincidence, his own countrymen were on the ground. He noted afterwards that he 'was particularly happy to see that the mission was in support of 1 Royal Canadian Regiment Battle Group, operating within Task Force Kandahar. There wasn't much going on in that area today, and most of the mission was spent searching roads for IEDs or anything else suspicious. However, despite the lack of "action", I was pretty pleased to be "supporting" Canadian soldiers on the ground.

'Another thing that I noticed on my first trip was how this part of Afghanistan is quite pretty, actually. It is not a whole lot like home, but it is kind of like parts of the States that I have flown in. It is very populated around Kandahar City, and all of the buildings and compounds look very similar. Just adjacent to Kandahar City are really neat mountains and sharp hills in almost all directions. South of KAF, there is a line in the sand that runs northwest-southeast that is the boundary between a "Red Desert" to the south and KAF and the city to the north. So, in its own right, this place is beautiful.'

Each day the ground forces from the whole of ISAF put their bids for air support to the Combined Air Operations Centre (CAOC) at Al Udeid, and it decided which units would receive it. Apart from manning GCAS, the squadron launched three pairs daily to cover the tasking from the CAOC. Typically, a pair of Tornados would be assigned to a JTAC to provide armed over-watch, much as they had been over Iraq, using the Litening III pod for surveillance and being ready to intervene directly if needed.

Over Afghanistan, the aircraft was fitted with a self-protection suite comprising the BOZ chaff and flare pod and BOL launcher rails, as had been the case over Iraq, but now the jet also carried a Terma Advanced Infra-Red Counter-Measures (AIRCM) pod, which gave further protection against man-portable SAMs. The usual weapons fit for an Operation *Herrick* sortie was two Paveway IVs and one or two DMS Brimstone missiles, as well as the gun. The accuracy of the Paveway IV was further enhanced by the ability to use hybrid laser/GPS guidance. The DMS Brimstone had also proven to be the ideal weapon in-theatre thanks to its accuracy, and also because the shaped-charge warhead limited its lethal effect to a very small area.

While operating as a pair, the Tornados flip-flopped between the tasking area and the tanker to ensure that at least one aircraft was always on scene. Within each aircraft, the pilot took responsibility for safety, deconfliction with other airspace users via the local air controller and kept track of the fuel state and the relative position of the tanker. The navigator communicated directly with the JTAC or FAC, and was the person who received the 'Nine-Line' – the legal authorisation to attack.

Sqn Ldr T Hill reckoned that each crew might expect at least one 'kinetic' event during their operational detachment, 'and that no matter your experience, you could still feel the hairs on the back of your neck standing up when you heard the "Nine-Line", knowing that this was for real, and that on the ground someone's life could be depending on you'.

By 2014, the typical weapon fit for Operation *Herrick* sorties included the DMS Brimstone as well as Paveway IV. Tornado GR 4 ZA587, photographed breaking away from its flight lead in August 2014, is carrying a single LGB and two DMS Brimstone missiles. It is also fitted with a Litening III pod (*Richard Hartley*)

In late October, another crew from No 14 Sqn used the gun for the first time in anger, having carried out their first SOF the previous night. They were No 2 of a pair that was providing overwatch for a routine night patrol in Kandahar Province for ISAF troops. 'We worked as pairs, only really splitting to pop to the tanker for some fuel', recalled the pilot. 'Whilst at the tanker, you would try and keep a radio on the JTAC's frequency to maintain some awareness of what was happening. Unfortunately, we were out of range, so refuelled and headed back to hear our formation mates taking a "Nine-Line" for a strafe attack!

'So, we arrived slightly on the back foot, trying to quickly get up to speed on the situation. The ground forces were taking fire from insurgents in a tree line, and they requested a strafe attack from each aircraft. RoE discussed and confirmed, Eddie and Dan were in first, and Jim and I followed about 30 seconds back. It was extremely dark, and although the NVGs helped, they were struggling with the low light levels. The navigators had the target on the Litening III pods, and once you were in the dive, as a pilot you had to have complete trust in the navigator, as the point he was marking was shown as a cross in the HUD. By day and on a good night you could obtain the target visually and adjust as required, but on this occasion it was a case of putting the strafe pipper in the cross and trying to fly the rest on numbers in the HUD!

'I saw the lead aircraft's rounds striking the ground and that helped confirm the location of the target area. I tipped into a 30-degree strafe attack and pulled the trigger. The gun fired and then stopped. In the split second it took to register this, the gun fired again, so I carried on down in the dive. I recovered at the minimum range as best as I could judge it, and the GPWS [Ground Proximity Warning System] warning went off, adding to the drama, with Jim shouting "Recover" from the back. I pulled 4g, with the nose at 15 degrees, and climbed up to safety. What a rush!

'The JTAC was satisfied with the result. The firing had stopped, enabling his troops to move into a better position. Our [time] with this JTAC was over, and we moved onto another area to provide overwatch – a much quieter area to the south of KAF, where the visibility was much improved. The troops were suspicious of some activity nearby and requested an SOF. We obliged, and the culprits disappeared, not to be seen again.'

When the Tornado was originally introduced into service, the heart of the machine was the Terrain Following Radar (TFR), and the night/all-weather capability that it endowed. Thirty years on, the TFR might have seemed to be archaic and out-dated by medium-level tactics and modern electro-optical equipment. However, in Afghanistan, the TFR provided the Tornado GR 4s of No 904 EAW with a uniquely useful capability. Amongst hills, and with weather or visibility frequently very restricted, it would be impossible for other types to get to low-level safely to perform a SOF, but the TFR provided an ideal way of doing so.

This technique was used to good effect on the nights of 3 and 8 November by Flt Lt J A J Robins-Walker, who confirmed that 'the TFR is as useful as it has ever been. To still achieve the effect of an SOF at night/IMC/very low light levels is invaluable, and was of great comfort to the Coalition troops. Although the SOF were flown over the flat terrain of Kandahar Province, both were on particularly dark nights, with low visibility due to mist/dust, in support of the Canadians to the southwest of KAF who were concerned about IED teams laying a trap for their route the following morning. The insurgents knew when the weather was poor at night there was less aerial activity, except for when the mighty Tornado GR 4 was down in the dust at 250 ft and 600 knots!

'Flt Lt Roughton was with me on both occasions, and we elected to use the TFR to get us down to 250 ft and then monitor with the NVGs, and if we could take over manually, it would allow us greater freedom to manoeuvre should there be any small arms fire. Our wingman provided overwatch by monitoring the area with the Litening III pod, and the JTAC had informed us of some large unlit masts in the area, so arranged a Line of Attack that would keep us clear of them. Even then, we felt a long way from the robust obstruction warning database available in the UK, so our eyes were on stalks for anything that the TFR might not pick up! During the sortie, we swapped roles, and our wingman also completed SOFs to maintain the noise and presence footprint for the duration of our time on station.'

One mission on 6 November illustrated how the technology of modern electro-optical targeting pods and precision-guided low collateral weapons had changed the face of CAS work over Afghanistan. A pair of Tornados was tasked to North Helmand to check out a High Value Target. 'It was the end of the day and night-time was closing in', recalled the pilot. 'There was also a UAV on station. We identified a vehicle with multiple personnel in it, but due to RoE constraints we couldn't strike without knowing who else was in the car, and whether we had permission to strike them also.

'We tracked the vehicle to several locations. Finally, we got the call to strike. We waited as the car approached and passed through villages, making its way through windy lanes and areas of high ground. We waited until there was an area we could strike in. Due to the difficulty of the terrain, it was hard to assess exactly when the best time would be to strike. On getting clearance, I waited for an opportune moment to release a DMS Brimstone.

'Unfortunately, on "tipping in" [to attack], the picture wasn't ideal due to some terrain masking the target. By the time it cleared I decided not to release, as we were approaching minimum range. I knew our No 2 would be lining up to support our attack behind us, and would be in a better position. I hauled off, called clear and [No 2] engaged with a DMS Brimstone. The target exploded and came to a halt, and at least three people managed to escape and started running in various directions. We positioned ourselves and engaged on the running individuals; we were now down to using the 27 mm cannon.

'This was a busy period, with aircraft repositioning in the air, switching height blocks and contacts. All of this whilst sorting out the targeting between the formation and carrying out individual weapon checks in order to carry out successful attacks.

'Our final pass was a strafing attack. Again, this is not a straightforward procedure at night and in mountainous terrain. The target sets were in the bottom of a valley, so a careful selection of [attack direction] was required. There are numerous things that can go wrong with such an attack, and the outcome can be anything from an aborted run to flying into the ground. The light levels were very poor, so based on the fact that we had a good

A pair of DMS Brimstone missiles mounted to the under-fuselage triple launcher (the centre station is empty). Developed by MBDA and declared fully operational (initially with No 31 Sqn) in December 2005, the DMS Brimstone proved to be an ideal weapon for counter-insurgency work in Afghanistan (*Chris Stradling*)

GPS position, I dived steeply at the floor in the centre of the valley. Stu was marking the target with the Litening III pod. We fired well over 100 rounds in the one pass. It was a busy, exhilarating and frantic period, the attack was a successful one and we returned home.

'The flight back was a period of personal reflection for me. I had conducted attacks before, but this was the first time I definitely knew I had taken someone's life. I'm not sure if everyone feels the same, [but] I think it is worth considering the fact that you have taken a life, how you think you should feel and how you actually feel. There are very few people in this country who are authorised to use lethal force, and even fewer who have to use it. It is something that will always be with you; it can never be taken back. Overall, it is a mixed feeling of doing the job that you have been trained to do, and the fact that rightly (or wrongly, depending on your viewpoint) you have taken a life.'

Non-kinetic techniques were often sufficient to persuade enemy groups to disengage from Coalition forces. Capt Janjua recalled an SOF near Anjir Shali, to the west of Sangin in Helmand Province, on 10 December;

'Shortly after starting work with [the JTAC] he informed us that they had just had an IED strike a convoy in his [area of responsibility]. He passed the coordinates and requested an SOF to ensure that any planned ambush of the convoy while it was stopped waiting for helicopter medevac of the wounded would be discouraged. "Macca" and I quickly sorted out the kit and airspace, and developed a reasonable plan. So, down we went to fly over the friendlies at 225 ft and 500 knots. We came off target into the sun for IRCM [Infra-Red Counter Measures], and "Macca" had the BOL pumping out the whole time at low-level.

'In the climb back to our working altitude, [the JTAC] informed us that the troops on the ground had heard AK-47 fire as we approached and flew overhead. Turns out the Taliban would take great pride in downing a fast jet with small arms fire; I guess that I can't blame them. The rest of this scenario involved us looking for bad dudes in adjacent compounds because the friendly FOB nearby was now taking a little [fire]. We couldn't ascertain positive identification, but we did see some suspicious groups moving around in tree lines.

'As we [left for the tanker], a British AH-64 approached to escort the medevac choppers and got a handover from us. After the flight, we reviewed the DVR [digital video recorder] footage from both Litening III pods. You could clearly see the convoy, stopped in its tracks as the lead vehicle has been disabled. We hoped that nobody was seriously injured.'

Ten days later, a pair of Tornados supported US forces in a mountainous area to the northwest of Kandahar as they attempted to head back to their base under the cover of darkness. The lead aircraft was on the tanker and No 2 was overhead the convoy when, in the pilot's words, 'all hell breaks loose and the convoy comes under heavy machine gun and mortar fire from the high ground to the north. [We] are requested to employ a Paveway IV onto the area where the fire is coming from, which we locate, but cannot make out any individuals.

'RoE and collateral damage estimate satisfied, I position the aircraft on an eight-to-ten mile run in. [My back-seater] is very busy marking the target with the Litening III pod, as individuals can now be seen firing down onto the convoy. We keep the laser firing on the Litening III, which is constantly updating the coordinates in the Paveway IV until release, when we stop the laser and let the bomb use GPS-aided navigation to hit the target. It is a direct hit, with the instantaneous fusing neutralising three insurgents and their weapons systems. The convoy is able to extract from the situation without further incident. [The navigator] did an excellent job in a high-tempo scenario with a very tricky target at night.'

1 January 2011 was just another working day, with a pair of Tornado GR 4s covering a US Navy SEALs team in southern Afghanistan. The Americans were particularly excited to hear the female voice of one of the navigators, and a low-level beat up of their compound also helped to bring some cheer to their remote outpost. Ten days later, Wg Cdr J K Frampton, commanding No 12 Sqn, took over responsibility for the Tornado detachment.

Although the pace of flying operations continued into 2011, the majority of kinetic strikes were now being made by Reaper RPVs, with the Tornados being employed for overwatch or RAPTOR reconnaissance missions. Crews might expect to be tasked for about three RAPTOR sorties each week, or perhaps to use the Litening III pod for Non-Traditional Intelligence Surveillance Reconnaissance. Again, these sorties were flown as pairs.

The reconnaissance role was far less exciting than 'going kinetic', but it was a vitally important job, nevertheless. 'This role never really made the headlines', explained a pilot from No 12 Sqn, 'but it saved countless lives due to the ability of the photographic interpreters to detect areas of disturbed earth along main roads, which would betray the presence of IEDs.

'One dark evening we were tasked to use the Litening III pod to provide top cover to a US Army counter-IED team. We spent two hours watching the Team gingerly do battle with a discarded 135 mm rocket turned into a deadly IED – a front row seat watching a scene from the *Hurt Locker*. Job complete, "Heartless 62" – the JTAC – asks us to do a sweep of the exit route for "nefarious activity" (a US JTAC's favourite expression for suspicious activity). Hey up, what's that in the middle of the road, a dark "splodge" on the infra-red Litening III picture betraying another 135 mm rocket buried in the dirt track. Indeed, more work for the team, but tremendous satisfaction that we played our part.'

By May, No 12 Sqn had been relieved by No 617 Sqn, commanded by Wg Cdr K Taylor, and the Tornado GR 4 crews carried out numerous RAPTOR missions over the district of Nahri Saraj, to the west of the Musa Qala River. This area, almost halfway between Kandahar and Camp Bastion, had the reputation for being the most violent corner of Afghanistan – the reconnaissance work was in preparation for a ground offensive there. On 26 May, a force of 22 helicopters, supported by overwatch from the Tornado GR 4s, delivered Afghan National Army (ANA) and Coalition troops into the village of Loy Mandeh to signal the start of Operation *Omid Haft*, the aim of which was to take back the region from the Taliban.

Meanwhile, in Britain, No 111 Sqn (the last Tornado F 3 unit) had been disbanded in April and two Tornado GR 4 units, Nos 13 and 14 Sqns, shared the same fate in June. In mid-2011, the Order of Battle of the RAF Tornado Force was as follows:

| RAF Air Command | | |
|---|---|---|
| Marham | No 2 Sqn | Tornado GR 4 |
| | No 9 Sqn | Tornado GR 4 |
| | No 31 Sqn | Tornado GR 4 |
| Lossiemouth | No 12 Sqn | Tornado GR 4 |
| | No 617 Sqn | Tornado GR 4 |

# OPERATION *ELLAMY*

In early March 2011, a UN Resolution authorised the enforcement of an NFZ over Libya, ostensibly to protect civilians from attack by the Gaddafi regime. Control over this operation was granted to NATO, and British involvement, which included both naval and air forces, was codenamed Operation *Ellamy*. The RAF contribution to the air contingent was ten Typhoon FGR 4s to enforce the NFZ and four Tornado GR 4s from No 9 Sqn, which deployed to Gioia del Colle, to carry out reconnaissance and attack missions.

Offensive operations over Libya started on 19 March when Coalition forces attacked air defence installations. The strike force included four Tornado GR 4s from No 9 Sqn that were armed with Storm Shadow missiles. These aircraft operated from their home base at Marham and completed a 3000-mile round trip, supported by VC10K and TriStar tankers. A second Storm Shadow mission by four Tornado GR 4s from No 13 Sqn was aborted shortly before weapons release for fear of hitting civilians in the target area. Three days later, another four Tornado GR 4s launched from Marham, and after flying an armed reconnaissance mission over Libya, they recovered to Gioia del Colle to join the Tornado detachment there.

While the Typhoons flew CAPs to enforce the NFZ, the Tornados flew armed reconnaissance sorties – both types worked closely with the Sentry and Sentinel ISTAR aircraft in-theatre. For offensive missions, the Sentinel played a central role in directing the attack aircraft by examining the areas of interest with its Synthetic Aperture Radar and identifying any potential targets, such as armoured vehicles or SAM systems. The positions of these were passed back to the Sentry, which in turn transmitted target details to the Tornados as they transited to the operational area. The Tornados could then use their own Litening III pod sensors to locate and identify targets and then engage them using Paveway IV LGBs or DMS Brimstone missiles.

Employing this mode of operation, Tornados used DMS Brimstone missiles to destroy three armoured vehicles near Misrata and two more further to the east in Ajdabiya on 25 March. Tornados accounted for a further 22 tanks, armoured vehicles and artillery pieces in the same locations over the next two days.

Another long-range mission was launched from Marham on the morning of 28 March to destroy ammunition bunkers in the Sabha area in the southern Libyan Desert. The aircraft, armed with Storm Shadow missiles, were refuelled by TriStar tankers during the mission.

Over the next few days, the Tornados targeted armoured vehicles, including main battle tanks, as well as SAM systems. The focus of operations shifted to Sirte on 2 April, and tanks and a number of armoured vehicles in the vicinity were destroyed by Tornados over the next few days, using Paveway IV and DMS Brimstone. The number of Tornados at Gioia del Colle rose to 12 on 6 April, but the most notable increase in ground-

attack capability was achieved by operating mixed formations of Tornados and Typhoons – the first such mission was flown on 7 April.

Armed reconnaissance missions continued over both Misrata and Ajdabiya during the first half of April, and on the 8th five tanks were destroyed. During the week a further four Tornado GR 4s deployed to Gioia del Colle, bringing the RAF contingent there to a combined strength of 22 Tornados and Typhoons. Mixed-type patrols continued, and on 18 April a Tornado and a Typhoon attacked a rocket launcher and an artillery piece near Misrata.

At the beginning of May, personnel from No 2 Sqn took over the Tornado GR 4 detachment from No 9 Sqn. On the 6th two Tornados attacked a concentration of FROG-7 and Scud ballistic missile systems near Sirte, destroying about 20 FROG launchers and damaging a number of Scud launchers. On the same day, Tornados also accounted for one tank, two armoured vehicles and a rocket launcher. Further attacks took place over the following days, including the bombing of a command bunker near Tarhuna by Tornados and Typhoons on 17 May.

The Libyan naval base at Al Khums, near Misrata, was attacked two days later. Tornados hit two corvettes in the harbour and also bombed a facility in the dockyard used for constructing inflatable fast attack craft. In a further series of air strikes on 24 and 25 May, Tornados and Typhoons targeted a coastal radar station at Brega, near Ajdibiya, and four heavy armoured vehicles at Zlitan, near Misrata. A Tornado dropped five Paveway IVs and a Typhoon four Enhanced Paveway IIs on point targets within a vehicle depot a Tiji, to the southwest of Tripoli.

After a break in the action of two-and-a-half months, on 10 August six Tornados carried out another long-range Storm Shadow strike from Marham, attacking Libyan command and control bunkers. Eight days later, Tornados operating from Gioia del Colle sunk a patrol craft transporting troops from the Az Zuwar oil refinery to the west of Tripoli. The following day, the responsibility for manning the Tornado detachment at Gioia del Colle passed once more to No 9 Sqn.

On the morning of 25 August, Tornado GR 4s located and destroyed a long-range SAM system near Al Watiya on the Tunisian border, and that afternoon a joint force of Tornados and Typhoons attacked a command and control facility near Tripoli airport. That night, a formation of Tornados flew from Marham to fire Storm Shadow missiles at a large headquarters bunker in Sirte. Once again, they were supported by AAR on this long-range mission.

This Tornado GR 4 taking off from Gioia del Colle on an Operation *Ellamy* sortie in the summer of 2011 is loaded with a pair of Storm Shadow cruise missiles on its shoulder pylons (*Crown Copyright/MoD*)

A fully armed Tornado GR 4 in its shelter at Kandahar (*Chris Stradling*)

Another Storm Shadow mission was flown from Marham on 14 September by Tornados supported by TriStar tankers. This time, the targets were vehicle depots and buildings near Sabha, in the southern Libyan Desert, which were being used by pro-Gaddafi mercenaries. The Storm Shadow strike was co-ordinated with another attack by Gioia-based Tornados, which fired 24 DMS Brimstone missiles at a formation of tanks and armoured vehicles near Sabha. Just over a week later, on the morning of 23 September, Tornados dropped 16 Paveway IV LGBs on point targets within a barracks and ammunition storage facility. The following day, a formation of Tornados destroyed a radar installation and control bunkers in Sirte with LGBs.

As Operation *Ellamy* wound down, the Typhoons returned to Coningsby on 26 September, leaving a force of 16 Tornado GR 4s at Gioia Del Colle. The NATO operation itself ended on 31 October 2011, by which time RAF aircraft had flown more than 3000 sorties over Libya – two-thirds of these were strike sorties. The Tornados returned to Marham on 1 November.

## OPERATION *HERRICK*

After a brief surge in operations in the last two weeks of 2011, air activity over Afghanistan had fallen into something of a routine during the early months of 2012 and the pace of British Army operations began to slow as more of the security functions were passed to the Afghan National Security Forces. For the Tornados of No 904 EAW, the tasking generally meant RAPTOR missions, with occasional SOFs or providing overwatch to search for IEDs ahead of convoys. Although some Tornado GCAS sorties were launched, many of them achieved their aims by an SOF rather than having to deliver weapons.

One such event took place on 20 April 2012, soon after No 12 Sqn had handed over in-theatre to No 617 Sqn. Two Tornado GR 4s had already spent three hours providing overwatch for troops in Helmand Province when they were tasked to attend a TIC near the Turkmenistan border some 300 miles away after a joint US/ANA patrol came under fire. A SOF by the Tornados at 500 knots was enough to persuade the insurgents to disperse, allowing the US/ANA patrol to disengage. The Tornados landed at Kandahar after a 7 hr 45 min sortie.

No 2 Sqn took over during the summer, flying more than 2000 hrs in support of British and Coalition forces, before handing over to No 9 Sqn. The last Tornado GR 4s in-theatre, flown by crews from No 31 Sqn, departed Kandahar on 10 November 2014.

The final Tornado units at Lossiemouth, Nos 12 and 617 Sqns, were disbanded in 2014. Thus, at the end of that year the Order of Battle of the RAF Tornado force was as follows;

| RAF Air Command | | |
|---|---|---|
| **No 1 Group** | | |
| Marham | No 2 Sqn | Tornado GR 4 |
| | No 9 Sqn | Tornado GR 4 |
| | No 31 Sqn | Tornado GR 4 |

## CHAPTER SIX

# IRAQ AND SYRIA 2014–19

## OPERATION *SHADER*

**B**y early 2014, a terrorist organisation known as Islamic State in the Levant (ISIL) had driven Iraqi government forces out of a number of cities in western Iraq. The group had already taken advantage of the chaos of the Syrian civil war to assume control of much of the northeastern region of that country, too. Many of the inhabitants of Iraqi towns and cities were displaced by the brutal ISIL regime, with the Yazidi population in the Sinjar area being particularly badly affected.

On 9 August two RAF C-130J Hercules transport aircraft dropped humanitarian aid to Yazidi refugees on Mount Sinjar. Six Tornado GR 4s from No 2 Sqn were then deployed to Akrotiri to assist with further drops. Supported by an RAF Airbus Voyager tanker, the Tornados were to use their Litening III targeting pods to direct the Hercules to safe drop zones on the mountain. Two more aid drops were carried out by Hercules on Mount Sinjar on 13 and 14 August, after which the Tornados were tasked for reconnaissance missions over northeastern Iraq, using the RAPTOR pod. Ten such missions were flown to gather intelligence about ISIL forces between 13 and 16 August.

From mid-September, the Tornado GR 4s started to fly regular reconnaissance sorties over Iraq. Operating from Akrotiri and equipped with the RAPTOR pod, the aircraft, still supported by the Voyager, flew in pairs, routing into western Iraq via Israel and Jordan. The British

Many Operation *Shader* sorties over Iraq and Syria started with a night take-off from Akrotiri, like this one photographed in late 2015 (*Richard Hartley*)

government authorised the use of weapons over Iraq in late September, and the RAF's offensive force at Akrotiri was augmented by two more Tornado GR 4s on 3 October.

As in Afghanistan, the aircraft were configured with the Litening III targeting pod and were armed with Paveway IV and DMS Brimstone – the first weapons were expended by Tornados on 30 September. Throughout the next six months the aircraft operated in support of the Iraqi Army in the city of Ramadi and the Kurdish Pershmerga forces fighting in northern Iraq.

Typical targets attacked by Tornados in Iraq included ISIL APCs, vehicles, artillery and mortar teams. The aircraft also disabled earthmoving equipment where it was being used to build improvised fortifications in ISIL-held areas. Tornado GR 4 crews typically expended live weapons on about ten sorties per month. Along with offensive operations over Iraq, surveillance sorties were also flown by both Tornado GR 4s and Reaper UAVs over Syria.

As with previous operations over Iraq and Afghanistan, each Tornado GR 4 squadron took its turn to provide personnel for a four-to-six-week detachment at Akrotiri. However, when No 2 Sqn converted to the Typhoon, leaving just Nos 9 and 31 Sqns to fulfil the operational needs over Iraq and Syria, another Tornado unit was needed to share the task. No 12 Sqn was therefore re-formed at Marham on 12 January 2015 under the command of Wg Cdr N S Thomas.

As one Tornado pilot recalled, 'the *Shader* detachments started to come round regularly – the only difference seemed to be a change in the areas of activity, as ISIL was slowly pushed out to the north and west. The names of Fallujah and Ramadi were all too familiar, just the enemy was different. We eventually moved up to Mosul. We started in the east and south of the city supporting friendly forces on the ground. The airspace was congested – the biggest threat to us was a mid-air collision with a Coalition aircraft or drone! The city looked huge from the air, and initially it was hard to tell there was a war going on. However, as the operation continued, you could easily identify those areas recently retaken'.

In early April 2015, intensive sorties were flown against ISIL forces preparing to attack Kurdish positions to the southwest of Mosul. The aircraft also flew overwatch missions ahead of advancing Kurdish troops to clear the area of IEDs and ambushes. Over the summer months, the focus of Iraqi Army operations in Anbar Province progressed from Bayji to Tal Afar and Fallujah. These ground offensives relied heavily on Coalition air support, including RAF Tornado GR 4s.

An example of the diversity of tasks carried out by Tornados over Iraq came on 23 July 2015. On that day, two Tornados on a CAS mission in support of Pershmerga forces near Sinjar used a Paveway IV LGB to destroy a building close to the frontline that was being used by a sniper engaging Kurdish forces. The aircraft were then called on to neutralise a mortar position, which they did using another Paveway IV.

Surveillance and CAS missions by Tornado GR 4s continued over northern and western Iraq through the summer, and a large number of weapons were expended. A typical day's work over Iraq in the autumn of 2015 is illustrated by operations on 25 November. During the morning, a pair of Tornados carried out attacks against three groups of ISIL fighters near Mosul using Paveway IV. They also destroyed an ISIL vehicle with a DMS

Brimstone, before moving westwards to neutralise a heavy machine gun post near Sinjar with a further Paveway IV. That night, a second pair of Tornados continued to support Kurdish forces in the Sinjar area, including destroying another heavy machine gun position.

By late 2015 the Tornado/RAPTOR combination was responsible for generating about two-thirds of the Coalition's gathered intelligence in Iraq. 'I am probably in a minority when I say that I quite enjoyed the challenge of flying these missions', commented Flt Lt Stradling, 'and I am modestly proud of

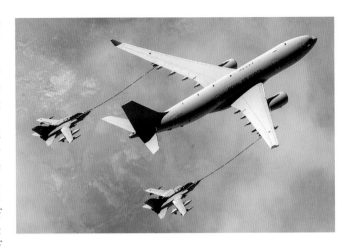

A pair of Tornado GR 4s refuel from an RAF Voyager KC 3 tanker over Iraq. During Operation *Shader*, Tornado force crews could take on fuel from a variety of assets supporting the fight against ISIL, including tankers from the Luftwaffe, the Royal Canadian Air Force, the *Armée de l'Air*, the *Aeronautica Militare* and the USAF, all of which regularly worked with RAF strike aircraft in-theatre (*US National Archive*)

the fact that I flew the very last RAPTOR mission with the Tornado. The pod was introduced in 2001, and has been used extensively, and with huge success, in both the Middle East and Afghanistan.

'The planning for a RAPTOR mission was considerably more complex and time consuming than normal CAS missions, and so it was almost always undertaken at least two days before the mission was flown. The flying was also more dynamic than routine missions, and required quite a lot of re-planning in the air in order to make the best of the time on task, collect all of the required points of interest and still fit in with the pre-planned AAR brackets.'

The British government authorised offensive operations over Syria on 1 December 2015, and the first of these was carried out the following day. Tornados attacked six wellheads in the Omar oilfield with Paveway IVs in order to disrupt ISIL's ability to fund its activities through oil revenue. The following day, the RAF's offensive force at Akrotiri, now designated as No 903 EAW, was further expanded by the deployment of two additional Tornados (bringing the total number in-theatre to ten) and six Typhoons. A mixed force of Tornados and Typhoons revisited the Omar oilfield on 4 December. That same day, Tornados and Typhoons flew CAS missions for Iraqi and Kurdish forces, and the latter also had CAS provided for them by a Reaper.

For much of December 2015 and January 2016, the Tornados and Typhoons provided CAS for Iraqi Army operations near Ramadi, as well as for Kurdish Pershmerga fighting near Mosul. On 23 December, two pairs of Tornados supporting Iraqi troops in action near the centre of Ramadi carried out six attacks on targets in close proximity to friendly forces. Using Paveway IVs, they neutralised three Rocket Propelled Grenade teams, a sniper and two groups in close combat with Iraqi troops. That evening, a further pair of Tornado GR 4s destroyed two buildings occupied by ISIL personnel near Mosul.

On 10 January 2016, pairs of Tornado GR 4s were operating near ISIL's self-proclaimed capital at Raqqa. One section attacked an ISIL command and control centre, while another section targeted a tunnel complex. A third patrol, working in co-ordination with a Reaper, used DMS Brimstone missiles to disable cranes and other heavy engineering equipment being used by ISIL to repair damage to the wellheads in the

Omar oilfield. Intensive air operations continued throughout early 2016 in the areas around Ramadi, Mosul and in northeastern Syria. Between January and March, Tornados mounted 52 air strikes over Iraq and 15 over Syria, using 147 Paveway IVs and 42 DMS Brimstone missiles.

From April, the region between Qayyarah and Hit provided a new focus for the Iraqi Army and, therefore, for RAF CAS operations. As part of a larger Coalition operation on 21 April, Tornado GR 4s dropped 2000-lb Enhanced Paveway IIIs on a tunnel and bunker complex on terraced hills above the River Euphrates. Tornados also used 1000-lb Enhanced Paveway IIs to destroy an ISIL command centre near Raqqa on 20 May and an IED factory in northern Syria ten days later. The final day of the month was also a busy one, with a pair of Tornados destroying two heavy machine gun positions that were engaging Iraqi troops advancing near Fallujah.

Storm Shadow long-range missiles were first employed against ISIL targets on 26 June when two Tornados fired four against a former Iraqi military bunker in western Iraq that ISIL was using as a weapons facility. Tornados also dropped Enhanced Paveway IIIs on 31 July while operating as part of a larger Coalition force attacking a Saddam Hussein-era palace complex on the banks of the Tigris River near Mosul that was being used as a major training facility by ISIL.

Meanwhile, Tornados, Typhoons and Reapers had been engaged in intensive operations over Manbij, supporting Syrian Democratic Forces (SDF) in northern Syria. They also worked closely with Iraqi forces in Sharqat and Qayyarah, in western Iraq, and Mosul, in northern Iraq. Operations also continued over the Omar oilfield – on 31 August, two Tornado GR 4s attacked tanker lorries attempting to transport oil from the area. Four Paveway IVs and four DMS Brimstone missiles were fired at the convoy, resulting in the destruction of a number of vehicles.

Most of the air support effort by RAF aircraft between October 2016 and July 2017 was focused around Mosul, where Iraqi forces were attempting to isolate the city from the southeast in conjunction with Kurdish forces operating to the north. Tornados, Typhoons and Reapers were all busy on a daily basis, working closely with ground forces.

'Urban Close Air Support was surgical but you couldn't help wonder about the poor civilians cowering under ISIL rule', wrote one pilot from

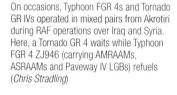

On occasions, Typhoon FGR 4s and Tornado GR IVs operated in mixed pairs from Akrotiri during RAF operations over Iraq and Syria. Here, a Tornado GR 4 waits while Typhoon FGR 4 ZJ946 (carrying AMRAAMs, ASRAAMs and Paveway IV LGBs) refuels (*Chris Stradling*)

No 9 Sqn. 'It was intense. You would come off the tanker post-transit and switch across to the JTAC and immediately be given a situation update, "Nine-line" and a game plan. Okay, heart pounding, chat within the formation, consider the RoE and your own game plan of how best to deliver the ordnance, maybe individually or as a formation.

'Invariably, drops were dangerously close (in the order of 60 m, one as close as 35 m for a DMS Brimstone) and in self-defence; listen out for the Ground Commander's initials (danger close, the GC accepts the risk) and final Target Engagement Authority. "Thump", weapon away, and manoeuvre the aircraft so that the navigator can keep eyes on. "Bang", sigh of relief, JTAC comes back and says Ground Commander's intent met. No matter how many times, there is that very nervous wait until that weapon is seen going to the intended impact point. The expectation was to be zero civilian casualties, and Coalition forces went to great lengths to achieve this.'

In addition, aircraft were tasked against insurgent and terrorist groups operating further south along the Euphrates River. On 31 October, two Tornado GR 4s participating in a Coalition air strike launched Storm Shadow missiles against bunkers at a former Iraqi military facility near Haditha. Meanwhile, the battle around Mosul continued into the following year. In November, No 12 Sqn took over responsibility for operations from No 31 Sqn and, despite poor weather in December, Tornado GR 4s still managed to provide precise air support to Iraqi ground forces as they fought their way into Mosul. The aircraft were able to drop Paveway II and IV LGBs through cloud with sufficient accuracy to destroy targets in very close proximity to friendly forces.

Eastern Mosul was captured by Iraqi forces on 24 January 2017, but the battle to clear the western half of the city raged on for another six months. Tornados, Typhoons and Reapers cut lines of communication to prevent ISIL reinforcements from reaching the battle, and they also cut roads within the city to stop the deployment of truck bombs.

'On several nights things got busy enough for us to clean the jets out of all weapons', recounted one Tornado navigator, 'and I fired my first DMS Brimstone against a vehicle-borne IED at night. The light and sound of the rocket departing was something else, and tracking the target was straightforward for a direct hit, which set off the device and caused a big blast.'

On almost every day, Tornado GR 4 crews were called upon to neutralise ISIL mortar teams and snipers both within the city and in outlying areas.

By early 2017, the Tornado GR 4 had been modified to incorporate the Link 16 Tactical Information Exchange Capability datalink and SCOT secure communications system. Sqn Ldr F J Macdonald of No 12 Sqn described a typical Tornado GR 4 sortie from Akrotiri during Operation *Shader* in early 2017;

'A flying day on *Shader* usually started with a ridiculously early start – regularly an 0100Z met brief. Planning a mission was quick, as we used data extraction tools to populate our briefing cards from the standing frequencies and ATO data. Some quick calculations gave us the take-off speeds, we printed the maps with the latest restrictions and we were then ready to brief. Met and Ops briefed us on arrival. Given the distances involved, in the winter we could encounter all sorts of horrendous meteorological crud between Akrotiri and Iraq or Syria. We were as heavy as we could be on departure, with a complete weapons and fuel load, so climbing above the weather was not always an option.

'Finally, we were ready to walk to the aircraft, usually with sufficient time to crew out and waddle for the spare. We were stocked up with lunch/dinner in the form of sandwiches and chocolate to keep us going for a whole day or night in the jet. It was a daunting walk, knowing you were about to strap in and go a long way in the next nine hours, never mind some of the things you would be asked to do; threats abounded, and they weren't necessarily shooting at you.

'Crew-in was slow, methodical and relaxed. The navigator was usually first in, having climbed up and checked the entire top surface of the jet – a "walkover" rather than a "walkround". With ground power on the jet, we could start the systems and test everything, weapons included. Once up and running, we waited for check-in time, having run through a detailed set of systems checks; bizarrely, the lights of downtown Limassol often glinted in the distance from the shelters, which always struck me as at odds with the operational mission we were off to conduct.

'Out to the runway on time and lined up as a pair, we powered up and checked all was well one last time. Lead rolled, pushing into "Combat" power with a roar which shook our jet and our teeth as they trundled off heavyweight down the 10,000-ft runway. Ten seconds later, we followed suit. Already, the Link 16 picture on the large screen in front of me showed us separating as we departed Akrotiri. We were essentially flying "airways" until we get into either Iraq or Syria, so ATC selected our departure time to avoid the local Cyprus airline traffic. Situational awareness was good in the GR 4. We could look on the "link" and see the aircraft in-theatre and the ones we would be replacing in the ROZ [Restricted Operations Zone], as well as what they were doing. So, we entered the area, having watched it for the past hour to build our picture.

'Into Iraq from Jordan, and we changed to secure comms, ready to meet the tanker. Now the fun began – it could be an Airbus A310 of the Luftwaffe or Canadian Air Force, an Italian B767, a UK Voyager or a US KC-135 or KC-10. Lots of ways to get fuel, some harder than others. Once we were topped off, it was time to transit to the operating area, handing off to the JTAC as we gained permission to enter and relieve our predecessors. The JTAC updated us on the picture, what had been going on, and what he wanted us to do. We set up our orbits, usually stacked in 100-ft height blocks for safety. Above and below us were other aircraft – A-10s, French Mirages, F-15s, F-16s, B-1Bs, all the way down to UAVs in the lowest blocks. It was busy, and everyone needed to be succinct and disciplined on the radio to keep the important stuff clear.

'We could be tasked with a variety of useful jobs, from watching "pattern of life" to trailing vehicles or conducting line searches along major roads. The JTAC had our feed and could see what we saw.

'A couple of hours into the VUL and it was time for more AAR. No 2 sorted the domestic radio calls, found the tanker and checked all was well. We drifted to the appropriate edge of the area and checked out with the JTAC. Now we could relax for ten minutes while we transited to the tanker; time for a pee and a bit to eat. Finding the tanker on the radar, we tracked him and joined up for fuel, which could take 10–20 minutes. Then it was back to the operating area for the second part of the VUL. If the day was quiet, we would not be called upon to drop, and could well be able to husband enough fuel to get home without a third AAR bracket.

'Once cleared to return to base, it was a long

A Tornado GR 4 breaks into the circuit at Akrotiri with wings swept back to 63 degrees following an Operation *Shader* sortie in July 2017. Two of the forward DMS Brimstone rounds have been fired during the course of the mission (*Richard Hartley*)

transit back, and time to finish our food and relax a bit. Once Cyprus appeared on the moving map display, we knew we were almost done. Back to the sun shelter seven or eight hours after we had left. With the canopy up, the breeze was fantastic and now Limassol looked good.'

Although the major part of the RAF missions in March 2017 were flown in support of operations in Mosul, reconnaissance sorties continued to be flown over Syria, and on 18 March an ISIL headquarters building was identified some five miles to the east of Raqqa. This was destroyed by a Tornado GR 4 that dropped a Paveway IV onto the target.

Tornados were also back in action over Raqqa in early June, destroying an armoured truck on its outskirts on the 2nd and neutralising sniper positions on the 9th, 11th and 14th. Two days later, a pair of Tornados destroyed a truck bomb factory at Al Mayadin, a town on the Euphrates River about 100 miles southeast of Raqqa. The building was demolished with a direct hit from a Paveway IV. These operations marked a change in emphasis from Mosul to Raqqa, reflecting the reduced needs of Iraqi and Kurdish forces, who finally took Mosul on 14 July.

Despite their defeat in Mosul, ISIL insurgent and terrorist groups were still active in northern and western Iraq. On 20 July, Tornados and Typhoons attacked an encampment on a wooded island on the Tigris River to the south of Qayyarah, and the following day a truck armed with a recoilless rifle was destroyed with a DMS Brimstone in a similar area. While operations continued daily over Raqqa, the Tornado GR 4s also provided CAS for Iraqi forces advancing westward from Mosul, neutralising mortar positions near Kisik on 16 August and Tal Afar the next day.

Operations were further west on 18 August when a Tornado/Typhoon mixed pair destroyed a booby-trapped building at Al Hasakah, in eastern Syria. Further south on 11 September, a Tornado GR 4 patrol attacked a terrorist group in a compound near Deir ez-Zur using a Paveway IV. When survivors of the attack then attempted to flee on a motorcycle, they were engaged with a DMS Brimstone.

Later in the month, while air operations continued daily over Raqqa, the Tornados also covered Iraq. A Tornado GR 4 destroyed an APC being used by ISIL near Qayyarah on 16 September, and another pair of Tornados destroyed an ISIL headquarters building and truck bomb factory near Rutbah on the same day. Between 20 and 23 September, the Tornado GR 4s operated in support of Iraqi forces to the west of Kirkuk, destroying ISIL strongpoints and buildings at Hawija and Al Sharqat.

In October, air activity over Raqqa diminished as the SDF took control of most of the city, and for the remainder of the year the Tornado GR 4s were generally used for armed reconnaissance missions over eastern Syria. On 9 December, the Iraqi government announced that it had regained control of all of its border with Syria, but aircraft stood by to assist in eliminating isolated ISIL groups that were still at large. That evening, Tornado GR 4s were called in to destroy a terrorist group that had been located about 40 miles northwest of Tikrit.

As the situation in western Iraq and eastern Syria stabilised, the tasking for the Tornado force wound down. Most of the missions in the next two months continued to be armed reconnaissance sorties over eastern Syria, often flown by Tornado-Typhoon mixed pairs. Kinetic events continued, but at a much-reduced rate. Reflecting the reduced tasking, No 12 Sqn was once again disbanded on 14 February 2018.

'In 2018, we also had to contend more with the Russian air force', wrote Sqn Ldr Macdonald, now serving with No 31 Sqn, 'particularly as *Shader* ops moved west into Syria. It's worth noting that at an operational level, the Coalition and the Russians were co-operating to deconflict. We were regularly intercepted by Russian Su-30s as we flew along the airways out of Akrotiri towards either Turkey or Israel. It was not uncommon to physically see "Frogfoot" ground attack aircraft operating adjacent to us, and we could track them on the Litening III pod to get an up-close view. On another occasion, I watched a long stream of "Backfire" bombers flying through Iraq from east to west and into Syria, all tracking on Link 16 as "unknown" tracks. Next trip out, I watched in fascination on the pod from east of the Euphrates as a "Backfire" unburdened itself of a full load of dumb bombs on the other side of the river.'

By mid-March, the operational focus had shifted once again to northern Iraq, and Tornado GR 4s were involved in mopping up operations, clearing ISIL groups that were attempting to re-establish an operational presence in the region. On 30 April Tornados mounted an attack on a tunnel complex on an island in the Tigris River to the south of Mosul, while a terrorist base in remote woodland to the south of Kirkuk was neutralised four days later. Another tunnel complex to the southwest of Mosul was attacked on 14 and 20 May. Other ISIL strongpoints, often isolated buildings or compounds in remote areas of northern Iraq or eastern Syria, were successfully attacked on 23, 30 and 31 May.

A No 31 Sqn pilot described how 'the last stand, literally, was in the middle Euphrates River valley. With the Russians and their fifth-generation fighters staunchly guarding the western side of the river, ISIS was fighting with their backs to the wall. On this day, there were aircraft stacked up every 1,000 ft from 12,000 ft to 25,000 ft, from fighters (including our Typhoon buddies) to ISTAR aircraft and UAVs, to the venerable B-1 bomber.

'All hell broke loose, the weather on the ground was poor and the enemy spied their chance of a counterattack. "Nine-line" after "Nine-line" followed from the JTACs on the ground. Stay clear of the Line-of-Attack of east-to-west in your height block and you would be safe. The threat was not from the ground but from hitting another Coalition aircraft – eyes out!! And do not cross the river.'

On 26 January 2019, a pair of Tornado GR 4s bombed five ISIL positions to the northeast of Al-Bukamal, which sits on Euphrates just inside the Syrian border. This was the last 'kinetic' event by the RAF Tornado force, and it was followed the next day by the last RAPTOR reconnaissance sortie. Sqn Ldr MacDonald 'had the fun of being on the last night op sortie in Iraq/Syria on Op *Shader*. And we had an easy one to see us out.

'Down on the Iraq/Syria/Jordan border, known as An Tamf, the Coalition had a large garrison charged with securing a vital three-border crossing which was widely used to move supplies and people into Syria. The garrison regularly needed convoy support to escort them around the area, and we picked up our fair share. An Tamf trips were short, due to it being a quick right turn into Jordan to pick up the airway and home without the need for a third refuelling bracket if you husbanded the fuel and delayed the second bracket. And so we were the last Tornado to exit Syria at night, forever.'

The final operational Tornado mission, flown on 31 January, was an armed reconnaissance by a pair led by Wg Cdrs J D Heeps and M J Bressani (commanding Nos 9 and 31 Sqns, respectively).

The last Tornado GR 4s left Akrotiri on 5 February. 'The formation transited north', recalled Flt Lt Stradling, 'and at 1300 hrs, over the mountains of Southern France, 4 hr 5 min after we got airborne from Cyprus, a message that I had pre-programmed into the aircraft's TV screens flashed at me to tell me that I had finally achieved my goal of 6000 flying hours on the Tornado. The flashing message also coincided with a congratulatory message over the radio from my squadron boss, who was in the lead aircraft of the formation.

'We landed at Marham five-and-a-half hours after leaving Cyprus, to be greeted by the most amazing reception, despite the atrocious weather. The Deputy Commander for Operations in the RAF and the Air Officer Commanding No 1 Group, accompanied by the RAF Marham Station Commander, were the first to walk up to the jets to welcome the crews back home'.

Chris Stradling had achieved the unequalled accomplishment of 6000 flying hours on the Tornado.

Following 28 years of continuous deployed operations post-Gulf War I, the Tornado finally left RAF service when Nos 9 and 31 Sqns were disbanded on 31 March 2019.

Flt Lt Chris Stradling achieved the unmatched achievement of 6000 flying hours on the Tornado during a career that encompassed operational deployments from Operation *Granby* (with No 17 Sqn) in 1991 to Operation *Shader* (with No 31 Sqn) in 2019. Overall, Flt Lt Stradling served with five operational Tornado units (Nos 12, 14, 17, 31 and 617 Sqns), as well as spending a number of years as an instructor with No 15 Sqn (*Chris Stradling*)

# APPENDICES

## COLOUR PLATES

### 1
### Tornado GR 1 ZA470/AJ-L (Operation *Jural*), Dhahran, Saudi Arabia, 1992

When the Tornado was first deployed for Operation *Jural*, the Desert Pink colour scheme reflected the belief that the sorties would be flown at low-level. The aircraft carries the markings of No 617 Sqn, and it is configured for a reconnaissance mission with a TIALD pod, 2250-litre underwing tanks, AIM-9Ls and the Skyshadow ECM pod.

### 2
### Tornado GR 1 ZA452/BP (Operation *Ingleton*), Dhahran, Saudi Arabia, 1993

From late 1992, replacement aircraft retained their grey/green camouflage. This jet from No 14 Sqn is configured for Operation *Ingleton* in early 1993, with three Paveway II LGBs under the fuselage, 2250-litre underwing tanks, AIM-9Ls and the BOZ-107 chaff and flare dispenser.

### 3
### Tornado GR 1A ZA395/N (Operation *Warden*), Incirlik, Turkey, 1996

This aircraft, in the markings of No 2 Sqn, is carrying the Vinten Vicon photographic reconnaissance pod, which became available from mid-1994. It allowed Tornado crews to obtain much better photographic coverage than was achievable via the TIALD video camera.

### 4
### Tornado GR 1B ZA457/AJ-J (Operation *Bolton*), Ali Al Salem, Kuwait, 1998

In the markings of No 617 Sqn, this Tornado GR 1B carries the white triangular fin flash and Union Jack that were applied to the aircraft deployed to AAS for Operational *Bolton* in 1998. The red-on-black caption below the cockpit reads *FLT LT D J H MALTBY DSO DFC*, who was the captain of the original 'AJ-J' Dambuster Lancaster. The aircraft also carried the name *SCOTCH BROTH* on the canopy rail.

### 5
### Tornado GR 1 ZA450/FB (Operation *Bolton*), Ali Al Salem, Kuwait, 1998

The standard stores configuration for Operation *Bolton* sorties included a TIALD pod and Paveway II LGBs, as well as 2250-litre underwing tanks, AIM-9Ls, Skyshadow and BOZ-107 pods. This aircraft is in the markings of No 12 Sqn. Some of the jets at AAS were named after soups, and this one carries the name *FRENCH ONION* on the canopy rail.

### 6
### Tornado GR 1B ZD716/JM (Operation *Bolton*), Ali Al Salem, Kuwait, 1998

The all-grey colour scheme was progressively introduced to the Tornado GR 1 in the late 1990s. At the same time, unit markings were reduced in size and limited to removable panels on the nose and tail so as to minimise repainting when aircraft were transferred between units. This jet is in the markings of No 17 Sqn.

### 7
### Tornado F 3 ZE808/FA of No 25 Sqn (Northern QRA), Leuchars, Scotland, 1993

Leeming-based units took their turn at manning Northern QRA at Leuchars. This Tornado F 3 from No 25 Sqn is armed with two Skyflash and two AIM-9L missiles, and it carries 2250-litre underwing tanks.

### 8
### Tornado F 3 ZG751/C of No 1435 Flight (Falklands Air Defence), Mount Pleasant, Falkland Islands, 1997

Tornado F 3 ZG751 from Mount Pleasant shows the markings of No 1435 Flight in the mid-1990s, including the coat of arms of the Falkland Islands. The blue and red bars on either side of the latter reflect the previous identity of the unit that was assigned this aircraft – No 23 Sqn. The jet is armed with Skyflash and AIM-9L missiles.

### 9
### Tornado F 3 ZG797/D of No 1435 Flight (Falklands Air Defence), Mount Pleasant, Falkland Islands, 2005

A Tornado F 3 in the revised markings of No 1435 Flight in the early 2000s. The aircraft is armed with AMRAAM and ASRAAM, the latter being mounted on BOL launcher rails. The TRD was not fitted and the aircraft were frequently flown, as depicted here, 'clean' without underwing tanks.

### 10
### Tornado F 3 ZE159/DE (Operation *Deny Flight*), Gioia del Colle, Italy, 1994

The markings of the previous unit (probably No 11 Sqn) have been crudely scrubbed out on this Tornado F 3, which was part of the No 43 Sqn detachment at Gioia del Colle for Operation *Deny Flight*, in the autumn of 1994. It is armed with four Skyflash and two AIM-9L missiles and carries a grey/green camouflaged 1500-litre tank formerly used by the Tornado GR 1 force.

### 11
### Tornado F 3 ZE834/ED (Operation *Deny Flight*), Gioia del Colle, Italy, 1993

A Tornado F 3 in the markings of No 23 Sqn operating from Gioia del Colle in 1993, shortly before the unit was disbanded. For Operation *Deny Flight* missions, the Tornado F 3 was armed with Skyflash and Sidewinders and carried a Phimat chaff pod on the outer stub pylon. This jet also has a Desert Pink 1500-litre tank inherited from Operation *Granby*.

### 12
### Tornado F 3 ZE810 (Operation *Resinate (South)*), Prince Sultan Air Base, Saudi Arabia, 2000

Outer wing pylons were fitted to the Tornado F 3s when they deployed on Operation *Resinate* in 1999 in order to accommodate the TRD. It was carried on the port wing, with a Phimat pod on the starboard wing, freeing up the outer stub pylons to carry AIM-9 Sidewinder AAMs. Note that unit markings were not routinely worn during Operation *Resinate* deployments.

## 13
### Tornado F 3 ZE962/XC of No 11 Sqn (Operation *Telic*), Prince Sultan Air Base, Saudi Arabia, 2003
During Operation *Telic* in 2003, the Tornado F 3s at PSAB were painted with the names of famous World War 2 fighter aces on their nosewheel doors (not visible when closed, as in this view). Some aircraft were also decorated with unofficial nose art. This jet, named *DEERE*, after New Zealander Alan Deere, still carries the markings of No 11 Sqn on the tail and is painted with *DENNIS THE MENACE* titling and artwork inspired by the *Beano* comic.

## 14
### Tornado F 3 ZE758/YI of No 111 Sqn (Operation *Telic*), Prince Sultan Air Base, Saudi Arabia, 2003
This Tornado F 3, named *CALDWELL* after Australian ace Clive 'Killer' Caldwell, originally served with No 111 Sqn. During the Operation *Telic* detachment as PSAB it was also decorated with a 'Tremble Shark' cartoon. The aircraft is armed with four Skyflash under the fuselage and four ASRAAM AAMs on the stub pylons, with the TRD and Phimat chaff pods on the outer wing pylons.

## 15
### Tornado F 3 ZE961/XD of No 11 Sqn (Operation *Solstice*), Šiauliai, Lithuania, 2004
This No 11 Sqn aircraft was one of four Tornado F 3s deployed to Šiauliai in 2004. Because of the short ranges involved in conducting Operation *Solstice* missions, the aircraft, which is armed with Slyflash and Sidewinder AAMs, is not equipped with underwing tanks.

## 16
### Tornado GR 1 ZA470/BQ of No 14 Sqn (Operation *Engadine*), Brüggen, Germany, 1999
In its new all-grey colour scheme with revised unit markings, this Tornado GR 1 from No 14 Sqn is shown in a typical Operation *Engadine* configuration in 1999. It carries two Paveway II LGBs and a TIALD pod, 2250-litre underwing tanks, AIM-9Ls and Skyshadow ECM pod. Yellow LGB silhouettes serve as a mission tally beneath the cockpit.

## 17
### Tornado GR 1 ZD810/DB of No 31 Sqn (Operation *Engadine*), Solenzara, Corsica, 1999
This Tornado GR 1 from No 31 Sqn, normally based at Brüggen, served with the unit's forward detachment at Solenzara during Operation *Engadine* in the summer of 1999. It is configured with three ALARM missiles beneath the fuselage and two more ALARMs loaded onto the underwing pylons.

## 18
### Tornado GR 4 ZD790 (Operation *Resinate (South)*), Ali Al Salem, Kuwait, 2002
Tornado GR 4 ZD790 was deployed by No 9 Sqn to AAS for Operation *Resinate (South)* in 2002. Bomb tally markings beneath the cockpit bear witness to the fact that weapons were expended

against Iraqi air defence systems on many occasions prior to hostilities with Iraq formally commencing in March 2003.

## 19
### Tornado GR 4 ZA542/DM (Operation *Telic*), Al Udeid, Qatar, 2003
Like the Tornado GR 1s of Operation *Granby* 12 years previously, the Tornado GR 4s deployed on Operation *Telic* in 2003 acquired unofficial nose artwork after their initial missions – female pin-ups were discouraged at the Al Udeid detachment. The artwork was based on the aircrafts' tail letters, so 'DM' from No 31 Sqn became *DANGER MOUSE* after a children's cartoon character from the 1980s. ZA542 was also christened *Dallas Dhu*.

## 20
### Tornado GR 4 ZA589/DN (Operation *Telic*), Ali Al Salem, Kuwait, 2003
Unlike the detachment at Al Udeid, which had been dissuaded from using 'pin-ups' for nose art, the detachment at AAS adorned its aircraft with paintings of scantily clad women. 'DN' of No 31 Sqn duly became the glamorous *DEADLY NIGHTSHADE*. The aircraft also carries a modest Combat Wing insignia on the tailfin, combining the badges of the Marham-based Nos 2, 9, 13 and 31 Sqns.

## 21
### Tornado GR 4 ZA554/BF (Operation *Telic*), Al Udeid, Qatar, 2003
The unofficial nose artwork on *BORN FIGHTER* again depicts the *Beano* comic character 'Dennis the Menace', and this time with the addition of his dog 'Gnasher'. The Combat Wing insignia on the tailfin denotes that the aircraft was initially deployed to AAS before transferring to Al Udeid. ZA554 is in a typical configuration for Operation *Telic*, being equipped with a TIALD pod on the forward left shoulder pylon and carrying two Paveway II LGBs.

## 22
### Tornado GR 4A ZA400/T (Operation *Telic*), Ali Al Salem, Kuwait, 2003
Just as the Tornado GR 1A had been used 12 years previously, the Tornado GR 4A reconnaissance variant was tasked with finding Scud missile launchers in Iraq's Western Desert during Operation *Telic*. Appropriately christened *Scud-Hunters*, ZA400 is also fitted with a RAPTOR pod for medium-level operations.

## 23
### Tornado GR 4 ZA553/DI (Operation *Telic*), Al Udeid, Qatar, 2004
Configured for a post-conflict reconnaissance mission over Iraq in 2004, this Tornado GR 4 is carrying a DJRP on its underfuselage centreline pylon. It is also equipped with BOL missile launchers on the inner stub pylons, but missiles were not loaded for post-conflict missions. Painted in the darker shade of grey adopted by the Tornado GR 4 force post-Operation *Telic*, ZA553 bears the insignia of No 31 Sqn.

## 24
### Tornado GR 4 ZA601/AK (Operation *Telic*), Al Udeid, Qatar, 2007
By 2007, the tactical situation had changed over Iraq, and Tornado GR 4s were often called upon to support ground forces. This aircraft,

in the markings of No 9 Sqn, is equipped with the Litening III targeting pod, DJRP and an Enhanced Paveway II LGB. ZA601 was the first Tornado GR 1 to be delivered to the newly formed No 617 Sqn on 23 April 1982.

## 25
### Tornado GR 4 ZA449/020 (Operation *Ellamy*), Gioia del Colle, Italy, 2011

Storm Shadow made its operational debut against targets in Libya during Operation *Ellamy* in 2011. Two rounds are loaded under the fuselage of this Tornado GR 4. By 2011, individual squadron code letters had been replaced by a Tornado GR 4 force-wide 'fleet number' on the tailfin.

## 26
### Tornado GR 4 ZA553/045 (Operation *Ellamy*), Gioia del Colle, Italy, 2011

This Tornado GR 4 also participated in Operation *Ellamy*, and it is depicted here in typical configuration for a sortie over Libya from Gioia del Colle in 2011. ZA553's self-defence suite includes ASRAAM missiles mounted on BOL launcher rails, the BOZ-107 chaff and flare dispenser and the Skyshadow ECM pod.

## 27
### Tornado GR 4 ZA609/072 (Operation *Herrick*), Kandahar, Afghanistan, 2010

This Tornado GR 4 was deployed to Kandahar for Operation *Herrick* sorties in 2010. Apart from a Litening III pod, it carries a single Paveway IV LGB and a single DMS Brimstone round. The markings of its former unit, the Fast Jet Weapons Operational Evaluation Unit (which merged with the Fast Jet Test Squadron on 1 April 2006), are still faintly visible on the tailfin.

## 28
### Tornado GR 4 ZA607/070 (Operation *Herrick*), Kandahar, Afghanistan, 2011

Like the DMS Brimstone missile, the 500-lb Paveway IV proved to be an ideal weapon for counter-insurgency operations. This Tornado GR 4 is armed with four Paveway IVs and equipped with a Litening III designator pod. Completing its stores fit are 1500-litre underwing tanks and BOL launcher rails. With no threat from radar-guided SAMs, the Tornado GR 4s operating over Afghanistan were equipped with the Advanced IR Countermeasures pod in lieu of an ECM pod. The T-shaped aerial protruding from the rear lower fuselage is for the CAGNET secure communications suite.

## 29
### Tornado GR 4 ZD744/092 (Operation *Shader*), Akrotiri, Cyprus, 2018

Tornado GR 4 tasking for Operation *Shader* included reconnaissance missions using the RAPTOR pod. This aircraft is depicted in early 2018, and in addition to the pod under its fuselage, ZD744 is also armed with Paveway IV LGBs in case it is re-tasked in flight to support ground forces.

## 30
### Tornado GR 4 ZA543/036 (Operation *Shader*), Akrotiri, Cyprus, 2018

This aircraft is depicted in what was probably a typical configuration for the Tornado GR 4 over both Afghanistan and Iraq/Syria during the final years of the jet's service with the RAF. It carries a Litening III pod and is armed with both Paveway IV LGBs on the shoulder pylons and DMS Brimstone missiles on the aft shoulder pylon. The self-defence suite includes the BOZ-107 pod on the starboard outer wing pylon and an AIRCM on the port side.

A top view of a Tornado GR 4 on an Operation *Shader* sortie over Iraq in May 2017. Between October 2016 and July 2017, RAF aircraft worked closely with Iraqi forces attempting to isolate Mosul from ISIL reinforcements (*Richard Hartley*)

# INDEX